J. H. E. (James Henry Edward) Secretan

To Klondyke and Back

A Journey Down the Yukon From its Source to its Mouth

J. H. E. (James Henry Edward) Secretan

To Klondyke and Back
A Journey Down the Yukon From its Source to its Mouth

ISBN/EAN: 9783744798730

Printed in Europe, USA, Canada, Australia, Japan

Cover: Foto ©Andreas Hilbeck / pixelio.de

More available books at **www.hansebooks.com**

TO KLONDYKE AND BACK

A JOURNEY DOWN THE YUKON

FROM ITS SOURCE TO ITS MOUTH

BY

J. H. E. SECRETAN, C.E.
OF OTTAWA

With Hints to Intending Prospectors

AND

Twenty-four Illustrations

LONDON
HURST AND BLACKETT, LIMITED
13, GREAT MARLBOROUGH STREET
1898
All rights reserved

DEDICATED

TO ALL THOSE WHOM I LEFT BEHIND

J. H. E. S.

INTRODUCTION

I have been advised by several friends—and some enemies—to write a book, describing the perils and pleasures which may be encountered in a voyage to the now celebrated Klondyke.

I have agreed to comply with the suggestion, purely from philanthropic motives—besides which I am given to understand there is money in it.

Should my feeble efforts be the means of preventing further immigration into that inhospitable region, and thus deter many an impecunious fellow-creature from either making a sudden fortune, or being miserably disappointed after much hardship and suffering, I shall not have laboured in vain.

CONTENTS

CHAPTER		PAGE
I.	TEMPTATION	1
II.	PREPARATION	7
III.	NAVIGATION	11
IV.	DAMNATION	16
V.	IRRIGATION	20
VI.	BOTHERATION	25
VII.	TRANSPORTATION	28
VIII.	ELEVATION	37
IX.	TRIBULATION	46
X.	DESOLATION	51
XI.	STAGNATION	57
XII.	EXHILARATION	63
XIII.	INUNDATION	68
XIV.	EMANCIPATION	74
XV.	CONTINUATION	78
XVI.	HESITATION	82
XVII.	ISOLATION	92
XVIII.	OCCUPATION	101

		PAGE
XIX.	PALPITATION	105
XX.	DISSIPATION	109
XXI.	PRIVATION	114
XXII.	EMIGRATION	129
XXIII.	EMBARKATION	134
XXIV.	INDIGNATION	137
XXV.	JUBILATION	148
XXVI.	COMMUNICATION	153
XXVII.	CIVILIZATION	157

APPENDIX	171
HINTS TO PROSPECTORS	176
A TABLE OF DISTANCES	216
MINING REGULATIONS	221
DREDGING FOR MINERALS	252
TIMBER REGULATIONS	259

LIST OF ILLUSTRATIONS

	PAGE
PORTRAIT OF AUTHOR	*Frontispiece*
FORTY MILE POST	3
FREIGHTER STARTING FROM CIRCLE CITY	4
MINING CLAIM, ELDORADO CREEK	5
GOING OVER THE CHILCOOT PASS	43
CHILCOOT PASS TWO-AND-HALF MILES FROM SUMMIT	45
LAKE LINDERMANN FIRST OPEN WATER	62
YUKON RIVER; ICE BREAKING UP IN THE SPRING	64
MILES CANON; LEWES RIVER	80
MILES CANON, LOOKING DOWN STREAM	82
MILES CANON, SCOW RUNNING DOWN	87
LOOKING DOWN STREAM TOWARDS THE DREAD 'WHITE HORSE'	89
THE DREAD 'WHITE HORSE'	91
SLEIGHING BOATS ON LAKE LA BARGE	95
MINERS ON THE WAY DOWN IN THE SPRING	107
DAWSON CITY	109

	PAGE
DAWSON CITY FROM OPPOSITE BANK OF THE YUKON	113
AUTHOR'S CAMP BELOW DAWSON CITY	114
INTERIOR OF TENT; AUTHOR WRITING DESPATCHES	116
AUTHOR'S CABIN, 'THE BEAR'S DEN'	119
RICH DIGGINGS ON BONANZA CREEK	132
NIGHT ON THE YUKON; END OF THE RUN	134
STEAMER 'JOHN J. HEALY,' YUKON RIVER	144
DOG TEAM, YUKON RIVER	193

TO KLONDYKE AND BACK

I

TEMPTATION

On a cold, cheerless day in the early spring of 1897, overcome by the persuasive eloquence of a respectable, though comparatively wealthy, syndicate, I decided to take charge of a small expedition bound for Klondyke. The main object was plunder. At this time it was not generally known that many rich diggings had been discovered in the vicinity of the Klondyke River, and upon the principle of 'first come, first served,' a soft snap was anticipated. In the event of a discovery being made, five men could control two thousand five hundred feet of creek bottom, and the result of the possible output, based upon what was already known to a select few, would soar serenely upwards into many millions.

In August, 1896, an inoffensive and unprogressive 'squaw-man,' rejoicing in the name of 'Stick George,' while building a fire on the banks of what is now Bonanza Creek, wherewith to cook his frugal supper, had accidentally thawed out the hitherto perpetually frozen gravel, and carelessly panned out *seven hundred dollars in coarse gold*. This amount provided the artless discoverer with a comfortable and protracted jag, which subsequently occupied much of his otherwise valuable time. During a lucid interval, this illus-

40-MILE POST. JUNCTION OF 40-MILE CREEK AND YUKON RIVER [*To face p. 3*]

trious individual, who, after the discovery, had adjourned to the more seductive attractions of Forty Mile Creek, where the old-time miner was pursuing his studies with varying success, electrified the little population one night by exhibiting the golden beauties 'big as beans.' Then followed the stampede.

From the little settlement of Forty Mile, all conditions of men loaded up their boats, and tumbled over each other in their haste to pole up the ever-rushing Yukon, fifty-two miles, to the promised land. It is related by the historians that men who had been harmlessly and painfully drunk for many moons were thrown into the bottom of the boats for ballast, later on to be used as stakeholders for claims destined to contain a million dollars worth of the precious metal; and everything on two legs that could scrape together a sufficient grub stake pointed the prow of its barque towards the new Eldorado.

Even after the dread Arctic winter set in, with its long dreary darkness, and the thermometer had casually meandered away down amongst the 'Sixties,' the news spread by some mysterious agency, and Circle City, hitherto a flourishing mining centre and distributing point, was deserted. A handful of women and children only were left to tell the tale of the 'has beens.' The men made their way up over the frozen surface of the mighty Yukon, many of them badly equipped and poorly provisioned, facing all the horrors of exposure in such a climate, helping each other onward towards the golden Klondyke, three hundred and fifty miles distant.

Bonanza Creek was rapidly staked from its source to its mouth; and the disap-

FREIGHTER STARTING FROM CIRCLE CITY FOR THE OUTSIDE WORLD.
1,000 MILE TRIP

MINING CLAIM. ELDORADO CREEK DRIFTING AND SLUICING [To face p. 5

pointed ones, who arrived too late, had to content themselves with claims on tributary streams, hoping that they too might turn out rich. Many a man passed by the mouth of Eldorado Creek with a sneer upon his face and contempt in his heart. Others, sooner than get nothing, took up a claim at haphazard on Eldorado, and the result has shown that all indications fail in this extraordinary country—for little 'Eldorado,' only seven miles long, a mere pup of the parent stream, has turned out the richer of the two.

This is briefly the history of the discovery of the now world-famed Klondyke, the marvellous wealth of which will some day, no doubt, astonish the universe and steal the reputation of all other placer mines, making them seem poor indeed.

Thus it was that I started upon my long weary journey, across the Continent, then up north from Victoria to Juneau, thence over the dreaded Chilcoot Pass, and after that through the wonderful chain of lakes forming the head waters of the mighty Yukon, ever rushing, contrary to all recognized precedent, straight north to the polar seas, there to belch forth mud and drift wood through a dozen mouths or more, covering one hundred miles, into the Arctic Ocean.

II

PREPARATION

On the 15th of April, at noon, the steamer *Topeka* sailed from Victoria, British Columbia, for Juneau, Alaska, with between two and three hundred passengers.

She was the first vessel engaged in the rush to the Yukon gold fields. Twenty-five mounted police and my little crew about represented the Canadian contingent. There was hardly standing room on the decks, and the berths simply would not go round. The ship was loaded down to her guards She carried a deck-load of lumber and a full cargo of supplies. On the upper deck many Yukon miners' sleds could be seen, and the melancholy howls of numerous half-breed Indian curs, down below, made up the complement of as mixed and motley a cargo as ever was seen. The rough-and-ready old miner, with gum boots and a steerage passage, strolled about hob-nobbing with some exiled scion of a noble family—blue overalls and black broad-cloth bunked down together. The lines were cast off, and the *Topeka* slipped away from the sunlight and warmth of Vancouver Island to wend her way through the picturesque archipelago stretching northward towards the shores of Alaska.

I did not go in this ship, but waited till the 25th for the steamer *Mexico*,* quite con-

---

* Since lost. She struck a rock and foundered in five hundred feet of water. No lives lost.

tent to linger a while and get a last whiff of the balmy spring breezes which float over this lovely island laden with the scent of jasmine, honeysuckle, and roses, before tackling the cold, uncharitable blasts of that far northern country.

I bought two Canadian Peterborough canoes in Victoria, also two gallons of Hudson's Bay rum—both very useful when mixed with water. And so, with little in the way of personal baggage, outside of a couple of pairs of blankets and two flannel shirts, I boarded the good ship *Mexico* on a Sunday morning. The church bells tinkled out their invitation to the righteous, the blue waters of the Pacific sparkled in the lovely sunlight, while the distant snow-capped mountains looked approvingly down upon a scene so calm and peaceful that nothing but the spirit of adventure strong within the human system could induce a man to calmly forsake it all and face the horrors of the north.

III

NAVIGATION

WHEN all goes well, nothing ever happens on a ship. In fine weather the time slips pleasantly by, and eating, smoking, and sleeping are the only available amusements. In these waters, the captain — usually of so much importance — has a sinecure. Two pilots take watch and watch and navigate the ship from one port to another, and it is only when she is entering or leaving a port that the captain is in evidence. It is then he puts on his brass-bound cap, and with a brief, 'I'll take her, sir,' telegraphs a few remarks to the engine-room, and lays his vessel alongside the wharf. The same thing occurs when leaving port—he backs her out, puts the helm hard over, swings her head round, while the pilot stands meekly beside him on the bridge, looking as unimportant as the father of brand-new twins in the presence of the monthly nurse. The captain says suddenly, 'You have her, sir,' and once again the pilot is monarch of all he surveys, and with a rumbling grunt, which sounds something like 'Noatheasbeasearfease,' he resumes his watch, while the captain goes below to scowl at the male passengers, and make himself agreeable to those of the female persuasion.

Within twenty-four hours of leaving the balmy air and soft sunshine of sleepy old Victoria, the *Mexico*, loaded down to the guards, was pointing her nose up against a stiff nor'-wester with a rattling accompaniment of hail and snow.

The steerage passengers were picturesque and very uncomfortable. One venerable gold-seeker told me he had a brindle cow for a pillow.

We had one celebrated cabin-passenger. It was a lady of marvellous development and wonderful experience. One cold wintry night, on the inhospitable shores of Cook's Inlet, this brave woman succeeded in rescuing, single-handed, either three or four, I forget which, shipwrecked mariners. She stripped off all superfluous clothing and plunged into the angry surf. The men were all unconscious, and like a big Newfoundland dog she dragged them ashore one at a time.

For this brave act she received several medals from different humane societies, and one from the President of the United States.

Withal, she was modest and unassuming, but distinctly ponderous. On one occasion, I came on deck, and asked her if she had seen a certain glacier, iceberg, or some little trifle of that kind which we had run past that afternoon. She replied with a sigh, and a pitiful disregard for Lindley Murray,

' No, cap, I di'n't. *I would so much like to have saw it.*'

She was a manly woman. I remember saying good-bye to her on board a small steamer bound for Cook's Inlet. The captain and I approached her most respectfully, and, as she grasped our hands firmly with that muscular life-saving apparatus of hers, the tears rolled down our cheeks, while she thanked us both for our great 'cordiality.'

IV

DAMNATION

We arrived at Juneau without incident on the 28th April, at ten p.m. That is what they call an all-night town, because everybody stays up all night and sleeps all day. About one a.m., in company with three ship captains, I visited the Juneau Opera House, situated in the rear of a huge bar-room, where all kinds of drinks and games of chance were dispensed freely. Faro, roulette, stud-poker, and craps were all in full swing when we arrived. I looked in vain for a box-office to buy a ticket, but soon discovered that no formality of that sort was insisted upon: you simply walked in and selected a box, of which there were plenty, and invested your surplus wealth in the numerous awful decoctions to be found at the bar. There were many ladies there, and with that wild western familiarity, so very charming, they strolled about in and out of the boxes, and chatted upon the political questions of the day, welcoming the stranger and putting the pilgrim at ease almost immediately.

The play was constructed to blend harmoniously with the surroundings. I did not at first quite follow the harrowing details of the plot, but eventually concluded the design was intended to illustrate at all costs that virtuous innocence was unsafe when inadvertently committed to the care of a ruined gambler for any length of time. A huge muscular giant, representing a miner, soon put all our doubts and fears to rest—also the ruined gambler—with the aid of a terrible-looking horse pistol. The play lasted till well on to the wee sma' hours, when the orchestra chairs were removed and dancing commenced, and was no doubt kept up with spirit by the ladies and gentlemen till breakfast-time.

But what a place of business, for all this: the beau ideal of an outfitting point, where everything requisite, from a needle to an anchor, can be bought. The miners' many wants are rapidly supplied in exchange for any sort of cash or convertible paper. The indispensable Yukon sleigh, suitable for either man or dog, flourishes in great profusion. The Yukon stove, which gets red-hot with so little provocation, and bakes your bread, fries your bacon, and dries your socks all at the same time, is also in great demand

Then we must have Mackinaw suits of many startling colours, good heavy blankets, the miner's kit of pick, shovel, and gold-pan, a full assortment of boat-building implements, which, with a generous supply of provisions, containing all the luxuries that we may luckily be able to afford, starts us on our way, if not rejoicing, at least secure from the perils of starvation for many months to come.

V

IRRIGATION

THE temperance people will be glad to hear that Alaska is a very strict prohibition territory; and yet the United States Government finds it necessary to employ numerous customs officials to collect duty on contraband whisky.

Licences are issued authorising the saloon-keepers to retail spirituous liquors, and if they are caught doing so they are heavily fined, at the same time paying a good big fee for their licence.

I heard of only one instance of confiscation: the offender, an over-zealous custom-house officer, was executed on the spot by the outraged whisky seller. Poor man! if he had only been content with inflicting a heavy fine upon the saloon-keeper, which he might easily have appropriated, he would have been living yet. But alas! this misguided official did his duty and paid the inevitable penalty.

It is considered a heinous crime to waste whisky in that country, and the sin is seldom overlooked or forgotten. Good business-like smugglers do very well up there.

When the miners come to town, they generally spare no expense to have a good time. I knew one good-natured giant, who, after indescribable toil, hardship, and misery for many weary moons, by strict attention to business had accumulated about *eighty thousand dollars*. The very best bad champagne was then only ten dollars a bottle, and yet it took this gentleman nearly twelve months to qualify for insolvency. He then went to work in the woods as an axeman, and a large Douglas fir-tree settled his future prospects by falling on him and breaking his back. They are a careless lot, and would be quite incompetent to direct the affairs of large monetary institutions, like the Bank of England, for instance. Let one of these men take hold of a concern like that for a few nights, when he was feeling pretty robust: the result might be quite disastrous in European financial circles. You see, he would not use the money to advantage when he had it.

They tell a story at Juneau of the discoverer after whom the town was christened. When he had made his pile, he came down from the mines, and, seeking out his favourite resting-place, sat down and actually wept bitter tears for fear that he would not 'live long enough to blow it all in.' It is a sad sight always to see a strong man weep; I have often read that in novels. However, old man Juneau had a better constitution than he anticipated, and is now working at the mines for two dollars a day and 'found.'

These facts only refer to the 'old timer.' There are many amateurs in the diggings nowadays, who are more careful, and save their dust for nobler objects than dancing girls, fire-water, and Faro banks. There are some, particularly amongst the Scandinavians, who seldom spend a cent. There are some who hoard their hard-earned wealth and are satisfied with a moderate-sized pile; then they go home, marry their sweethearts, settle down, and sell beer for the rest of their lives. I knew one little German who suffered untold miseries in the frozen north for years. He had gone through successive stages of scurvy until he had almost lost heart, together with all his front teeth. He also had asthma, so that he could hardly carry his fifty pounds of dust, packed up in a raisin box, without resting every few steps. And yet this hundred thousand dollar invalid had visions of happiness, because one day he confided in me (I seem to invite these confidences from rich people) that when he got 'owat' he would buy him a bunch of grapes for five cents, in New York, *every day*. I did not hear whether he persevered in this extravagance.

VI

BOTHERATION

It is not far to Dyea from Juneau—only one hundred miles by sea; but the available transportation facilities, although numerous, were decidedly uncomfortable and alarming.

My merry men had gone up with the now North-West dismounted policemen in a wonderful construction called the *Gasoline*. This craft seemed to be a direct descendant of Noah's Ark, and equally populous. It had a small gasoline engine concealed about its person somewhere, and a record of four miles an hour.

Imagine, if you can, thirty-five robust adults, with all their camping paraphernalia, equipment, and provisions, embarked on board this little ship, only to discover that the mate was in liquor and the captain in gaol. This caused a certain amount of delay; first, the boat had to be baled out, then the captain—and I have no doubt the mate would have felt better for a similar attention.

They told me the captain, a piratical-looking ruffian, came on board late in the evening, consumed with alternate threats of vengeance and maudlin repentance. He was easily distinguishable from the other officers on account of a black eye.

Dyea lies at the head of the Lynn Canal, and at this time consisted of Healy and Wilson's trading post and the 'Klondyke Saloon.' The little *Gasoline*, with its cargo of humanity, at ten dollars per human, was cut loose and fretted along with a good deal of clicketty-clack, making for the point of Douglas Island, several miles from Juneau. The miserable passengers distributed themselves as best they could amidst the baggage, as there was only room for a paltry half-dozen in the wretched little dimly-lighted cabin. The little gasoline engine generously diffused a powerful bouquet over everybody and everything, and a good steady rain made everybody happy and very wet. In a few hours the motive power ran out, and there was nothing for it but to hoist the sails. A favourable southerly breeze was all the luck they had, and, after running before it all night 'wing and wing,' Dyea was sighted in the morning.

VII

TRANSPORTATION

Before leaving the very last remnant of civilization, I paid a visit to the celebrated Treadwell mine on Douglas Island, a few miles from Juneau. The good ship *Mexico*, Captain Thomas, dropped down there during the alleged night. We had a deck-load of timber for the mine and a couple of big iron boilers. The deck-load was easily disposed of in the picturesque way they do things in Alaska, by simply chucking it overboard and allowing the consignee the privilege of picking it up if he could—much on the same principle as Josh Billings, being in a commercial frame of mind, is supposed to have written to his wife:

'My dear wife,—Enclosed please find ten dollars, if you can.'

I waited patiently on deck to see whether they would land the boilers the same way, and felt quite disappointed when they did not. I was introduced to the manager and the mine, and heard the continuous pounding of the two hundred and forty stamps and other machinery which, night and day all the year round, except Christmas Day, crunches up the rock and extracts the precious yellow metal for the benefit of the lucky shareholders.

The cargo unloaded, we were soon back at Juneau alongside the wharf. I cannot help thinking that this wharf must be a source of much revenue. The proprietors, whoever they are, do not neglect to charge anyone who may be compelled to patronize them. I only wonder they do not publish a tariff for the benefit of the 'pilgrims,' which would read about like this:—

	dollars.	cents.
Looking at wharf	1	00
Breathing on wharf	1	75
Spitting on wharf	2	00
Stepping on wharf	2	50
Speaking to a man who said he knew the wharf	2	75
Placing valise on wharf	3	00
Removing valise from wharf	4	00

I think if a passenger landed with a gripsack in each hand, and managed to walk across the wharf without attracting attention, they might let him off free. He would of course be permitted to carry an umbrella in his teeth.

I innocently landed my two canoes, and 'tis true they remained there overnight, occupying a double-bedded shed, without any pretension to luxury or comfort. There was not even a looking-glass in the place, and it was far from being an ideal marine bridal chamber; but when I went to get my poor innocents next morning there was a formidable yellow document setting forth that so many cubic feet, calculated by Greenwich time, in 129° west longitude, and multiplied by the management, plus the commission of all the clerks, was equal to the tonnage of a first-class cruiser, which at so much a ton amounted to exactly twice the value of the canoes.

Taking in the situation at a glance, 1 offered to surrender the canoes and give them my note for the balance. I once heard of a man who was said to be mean, because he tried to get into a circus half-price, on the ground that he had *only one eye*.

The irregular fleet which was supposed to ply between Juneau and Dyea, consisted of the *Bustler*, which was certainly the flagship, the *Gasoline*, and the *Alert*. I selected the latter for several reasons, the principal one being that the other two, like an after-dinner speaker, were 'too full for utterance.' Another thing made me fancy the *Alert*. I had discovered that, out of the dozen or more men who had engaged passage in her, there were not more than six or seven sober enough to distinguish a steamboat from a cow, so that I hoped for comparative comfort and less crowding.

Alas! there were *seven* passengers, and we were crowded. The little craft buzzed merrily along, occasionally dropping a hat or a trunk overboard, to kind of blaze the way back.

The crew consisted of a very small boy, who I think would have been bright, but he had not been washed that spring. He was stoker, stevedore and, I regret to say, *cook*. He also steered the boat when he was not busy.

Our only meal on this passage apparently consisted of pork chops on the half shell, bread, with unmistakable dusky signs of the young gentleman of the first part, and opaque tepid water which had evidently been trying to get up a flirtation with a pinch of green tea and had been bitterly disappointed.

It was lonely work, and there was nothing to do but watch the porpoises and hang on to the little ship in fear and trembling. The night was long and weary, but there was no place long enough to lie down upon. The captain, having bent on a line to the little watch-charm anchor, suddenly let it go at four a.m. in six fathoms of water. I could not understand this at first, but soon after I solved the mystery in a very practical manner. We were only drawing six *feet*, and I wondered why we anchored in six *fathoms*. It was chilly and very desolate at that time in the morning, and a cold damp sea fog closed in upon us to make the gloom, oh! so beautifully complete. I bethought me of the two tiny canoes, roosting peacefully in their respective crates on the boiler top, and, securing a fellow-sufferer, proceeded to launch my frail barque and tried to make the land. It did not take long to discover that a thirty-five foot ebb-tide had an important engagement that morning down town. I gave orders to take soundings, and seven inches by the mark was the melancholy discovery. This rapidly shoaled to four, which compelled us to abandon the ship a good mile from the shore proper. So we picked her up on our shoulders and marched wearily over the long dreary mud-flats in the direction of Healy and Wilson's store.

I was lucky here. Arriving at my initial point, cold, wet, weary and hungry, I ran across an old pioneer, who like myself had seen strange things before. With true hospitality, begotten of a long western residence on the plains, Sam Heron took me in and, reaching under the bed, produced a bottle. I meekly asked for a cup, and even went so far as to suggest water; but seeing the gathering sneer upon his surprised Alaskan countenance, I shut my eyes and commended myself to heaven, took a short sharp pull, and think I must have dislocated my left lung. Shortly afterwards, when I had stopped coughing, I thanked him most cordially with tears in my eyes. He was very glad to see me, and it was difficult to prevent another pyrotechnical experiment out of the same bottle.

VIII

ELEVATION

I do not know whether you have ever witnessed a 'rush to the gold-diggings,' and been well mixed up in it yourself. If not, it is an experience that I could not recommend. There are many other pleasanter ways of putting in time.

I have seen a nice, steady-going, respectable member of society in comfortable circumstances calmly pursuing the calling which he had adopted, with fair chances of moderate success and comparative happiness. Yes, I might almost add to these attractions a pretty wife and the usual little footsteps. This individual is apparently quite sane enough for all practical purposes, and would never think of robbing a bank; when some day a wandering prospector turns up and exhibits a handful of nuggets, worth perhaps two hundred dollars. I have watched the calm blue eye of the respectable member of society aforesaid suddenly flash with the glitter of avarice, as he fondly fumbles the little yellow chunks and meditatively weighs them in his hand. In a moment the pretty wife, the fairy footsteps, the regular salary, the happy home with the framed text over the mantelpiece, are all forgotten. A wild, insatiable lust after lucre takes possession of this poor but honest haberdasher, and he longs to go and do likewise. All it takes now is the hurried perusal of a pamphlet, ' Advice to Gold Seekers,' or a Transportation Company's folder, with glowing descriptions of ' gold dust plentiful as sawdust,' or some equally glittering lie; and he is a lost soul. The modest little home is hastily given up, he scrapes together his few hard-earned ducats, and, with a blue flannel shirt on his back and an incipient beard on his chin, he joins the misguided motley procession.

Another phase of the disease, when the germs are once absorbed into the system, is that no antidote has ever yet been discovered. I have met many victims on the road to disappointment and destruction, and, in language begotten of experience and faltering with well-feigned emotion, I have lamentably failed to persuade them to turn back ere it was too late. I have heard old chuckle-headed parents proudly announce with assurance, the offspring of ignorance, that though the heavens fall 'our John will get there.'

At Dyea on the 1st of May, 1896, a thousand people, men, women, children, and unweaned babies, were struggling to get over the Chilcoot Pass. There were many dogs and several Indians to help them.

I soon learned the whereabouts of my little force. Surrounded by every conceivable species of human being, of all shades and nationality, they were camped at the mouth of the Dyea Cañon, the entrance to the Chilcoot Pass. This is only about nine miles from the sea, but it is no joke to take even three tons of supplies that far. My people did it by hastily building small flat-bottomed boats fifteen feet long, which they loaded and dragged up the shallow glacier stream called the Dyea River, a distance of six miles. Here navigation ends and everything has to be carried. The coast-range Indian is no doubt a wonderful beast of burden, and very useful to man. At ten cents a pound, he will stagger over mountain passes with a load on his back that makes you tired to look at or pay for. He is teetotally unreliable, and will drop your most precious belongings anywhere, upon the slightest provocation of another cent from the first stranger he meets. But he is a very necessary ruffian until the Chilcoot Pass is abolished.

I was anxious to ascertain if the pass was really as heartrending as the pictures I had seen in the guide-books portrayed it, and consulted an American gentleman who came up in the *Alert* with me, and who subsequently had been industriously earning a ' grub stake ' by packing up to the summit. I simply asked him if it was as steep as represented. He had a wan, pale, drawn look, and after reflectively scratching his ear he said,

'Wal, cap, I was *pre*-pared for it to be per-*pen*-dicular, but by G——d I never thought it would *lean back*.'

To surmount the Chilcoot Pass and the attendant difficulties, it is most essential to secure a fine day. These phenomena are very scarce. It is not uncommon for three weeks to elapse before the weather is sufficiently calm to ensure a safe passage.

To feebly illustrate this, two of my men had been sent across the summit to Lake Lindermann, while two remained to bring up the last of the camp equipage. These latter two, failing to get across the next day, were separated from their companions for a week, as there was no fine weather during the interval.

GOING OVER THE CHILCOOT PASS

The day I crossed, May 8th, it was raining on the southern, can I say *slope*, in the early morning; but this rapidly changed to snow when I was at the foot of the summit and *it commenced to blow*, as is usual, from the south. I fancied that I had often heard it blow before. I have assisted at a western tornado, and been present during the first act of a Minnesota cyclone. I have also heard a patriotic orator air his eloquence on the Fourth of July. But all this experience faded into insignificance when this little southern zephyr announced its birth with a wild, mad, howling shriek. You could lean up against it.

With bewildering rapidity the air became filled with particles of whirling snow, and in less than five minutes I could only faintly distinguish the heels of the man immediately ahead of me, which I remarked were generally on a level with my eye, and I could not help thinking of the words of that well-known song, so appropriate to this occasion, 'The blow it near killed father.'

Some enterprising individual had established a wire cable for the last six hundred foot lift, worked by two poor wretched horses, who were patiently plodding round in a circle, winding up sleigh-loads of supplies and passengers at one and one-half cents a pound. I heard casually that this gentleman was clearing one hundred and fifty dollars a day by the operation.

I saw one unfortunate woman perched on top of a loaded sleigh, ready to make the ascent. She was seated with her back to the scenery, and then they passed the baby up to her to take charge of. But this was too much for her, and I

CHILCOOT PASS 2½ MILES FROM SUMMIT

heard her distinctly refuse to 'resk the life of the child;' and so the juvenile Yukoner was carried up by one of the men as the careful mother slowly ascended the almost perpendicular height and disappeared into the clouds.

The maternal instinct is certainly sometimes wonderfully developed, particularly in woman.

IX

TRIBULATION

ONCE at the summit of the Chilcoot Pass, three thousand five hundred feet above the sea, crowded into such a short horizontal space, the danger and difficulties ahead appear to dwindle into insignificance. Elevation having been accomplished, elation follows, and the downgrade plunge is most welcome, but how it did storm up there!

Far above the timber line, without shelter, it is a very wise move to seek the lower levels as rapidly as possible.

There is little difficulty in this, as the descent on the northern side is almost as abrupt as the southerly approach. It is about five hundred feet vertically to Crater Lake, and not much more horizontally. The usual method of getting there is to sit down suddenly on the summit. You have arrived when you stop. The summit is not the sort of place to linger at. There are no attractions of any kind. Many tons of supplies, however, have to be left there to the tender mercies of the elements, till you can send back for them, sometimes only to find them buried deep beneath the drifted snow, when, after prodding carefully round in the supposed vicinity, you may be able to locate your provisions and dig them out. The day I crossed, an enterprising dentist bound for Dawson City lost his whole kit of tools, and never recovered them.

The wind comes roaring down through the pass, the dazzling glare of the sun reflected from the snow literally tears the skin off your face, the exertion of continuous climbing throws you into a violent perspiration, and, when you stop for a moment to collect your thoughts and breath, the icy blast strikes through your very marrow, chilling you to the core. Visions of pneumonia and other kindred complaints flit through your bewildered brain, with the accompanying panorama of a highly respectable funeral procession, as you wearily drag one leg after another, and make affidavits with yourself that this shall never occur again. It is true that there are distinctly discouraging moments in the vicinity of the summit.

Only nine miles to Lake Lindermann, the very head waters of the Lewes, Pelly,

Yukon Waterway, and all down-hill. After miles and miles of ten steps and a breather, the luxury of a few hundred feet of level can hardly be explained. If it is only a slight incline, which in civilized society would undoubtedly be regarded as quite steep, it feels like going down-hill, such is the comparative effect.

From the summit to Lake Lindermann has been described by one well-meaning historian as ' only a pleasant run.' I envy him his powers of description. It is a mistake to bring people up to middle age with an idea that it is the correct thing to tell the truth.

I did not try ' a pleasant run,' although the pamphleteer distinctly promised it, but I have a large-sized impression of having accomplished a very unpleasant walk, through chains of frozen lakes, over ridges, down valleys clothed in soft mushy snow, beneath icy precipices, till at last Lake Lindermann hove in sight.

This might all have been considered a pleasant run if the conditions had been favourable; but, alas! in my case, the snow was melting, the ice was marked dangerous, the cañon was reported impassable, and altogether there was nothing very pleasant except the novel sensation of once more going down-hill.

X

DESOLATION

AND thus followed my banishment. Twenty-one long desolate days and dreary nights, camped upon a gravel bar at the head of the lake, profusely decorated with boulders of all sorts and sizes, surrounded by a human mob of most diverse professions, all anxious to reach the golden Mecca to ply their varied trades and indulge in their different avocations for the benefit or ruin of the honest, innocent miner.

Misery likes company, and poverty makes strange bed-fellows. These two well-worn adages are most appropriate in a stampede of this kind. The 'right sort' assist each other in difficulties which of course cannot be experienced in civilization. It is when the grim monster has to be faced and a timely stroke of the paddle averts calamity, or a kindly helping hand snatches us from a fatal header into some fathomless abyss, that the true qualities of men come to the front and can be really appreciated.

Charity too, and the general principle of 'dividing up,' is most conspicuous amongst those who get accustomed to suffer untold hardship together.

I was surrounded by contraband whisky pedlers, gamblers, Jews, Gentiles, ladies whose briefness of skirt barely equalled the briefness of their characters, old miners, young gentlemen, escaping murderers, returning Yukoners, safe in the happy possession of rich claims, always oracles to be looked up to and respected.

'See that old fellow over there with them two black dorgs, that's his wife with him, say he owns twenty-eight Eldorado, he took out sixty thousand dollars last year and went after his wife;' and the chances are you would see as miserable a specimen of the genus homo as ever disgraced a pair of blue overalls.

I struck up quite a comradeship with a small wiry Israelite, who was taking in a mixed cargo of whisky, supplies, and clothing. He invariably addressed me as 'Cap,' but at other times, when not in a familiar vein, he would call me 'Mr. Sextant,' evidently looking at the two as being synonymous from a nautical point of view.

He had been over this route several times before, and had made a trip from Circle City to Dyea, something over a thousand miles, on the ice in the dead of winter. He had thirteen dogs, five men, and a partner with him. The dogs were beauties. My favourite was surnamed 'Shaggs,' on account of the immense crop of wool he possessed. There was no doubt in my mind that some of his ancestors had been indirectly compromised by a black bear. He had a perfect bear's head; he was absolutely black, with a white spot over each eyebrow; the wool upon his forehead was about eight inches thick, and he was always on the broad grin. He was the handsomest dog and the most nondescript I ever saw.

'Shaggs' had a chum in the team who rejoiced in the name of 'Ginger.' He was the ugliest animal imaginable. His ancestors seemed to have had the same difficulty with the bear family, evidently being more partial to the Cinnamon variety.

These two were inseparable. They worked together all day, ate together in the evening, and slept together at night. 'Ginger' played Damon to perfection, while old 'Shaggs' was an exemplary Pythias. Woe betide the dog that indulged in any breach of etiquette at dinner time, or attempted any familiarity with either of the 'pardners.' The gentle smile would fade from the lips of 'Shaggs,' and with a low threatening growl he would warn the intruder to retire. This was generally sufficient.

There were many other splendid specimens in this train, 'Bob,' 'Charley,' 'White Horse,' 'Jack,' and little 'Yukon,' the leader, a native born dog, a smug-faced little beast, jet-black with a perfect white collar, and on account of this and his innocent inane expression, so often found in curates, we christened him 'the parson.'

On many a stormy night, when the wind was howling and the snow drifting, the little stove-pipe rattling, and the tent surging and trying to break away from its moorings, I have noticed my friend 'the parson' quietly insinuate himself into the shelter and meekly sit bolt upright before the remnants of the fire, looking the picture of genteel poverty, with a beseeching expression almost human, which plainly said, 'I hope I don't intrude'—while outside in the howling blast, a large black ball of wool and a similar one of yellow, close together, located the position of the sleeping 'pardners.'

XI

STAGNATION

THREE weeks is a long pause, made compulsory by stormy weather on the summit of the coquettish Chilcoot, where the Goddess of Wind, if there is such a virago, would gently flirt her fan for a moment and obliterate the landscape; where strong men would slave and toil for weeks harnessed to sleighs loaded with the necessaries of life, ever struggling onward towards the golden goal, the faint-hearted often turning back in disgust, the stronger and more aggressive persevering in their self-imposed task, only perhaps to meet a watery grave beyond.

There was much food for reflection for a philosopher at the head of Lake Lindermann, if nothing else. The little camp was daily increased by the arrival of many curiosities, all hopeful and absolutely positive of success. As the sun rose earlier each day and set later each night, he rapidly gained on the ice-encrusted scenery, and rendered travelling over the lake uncertain and unsafe. There was nothing for it but to wait. Impatience to reach the mines had to be curbed in deference to the physical conditions of the climate.

Many variety women, taken in by polygamous bar-tenders, began to arrive. An occasional broken-down comedian, with a tired expression and an assortment of well-worn clothes and jokes, would swell the merry multitude, and make the short night hideous with piteous appeals to 'Just tell me that you love me,' etc. : an absolute impossibility under the circumstances.

Amidst all the grotesque features of this combination, there could always be seen the profoundly pathetic side of life. I remember one poor unfortunate woman, who had accompanied her husband, and brought the new-born baby along, sooner than leave him to the care of strangers, after having successfully dragged herself and the boy across the icy barrier, was fated to pursue her weary journey with heavy heart, and eyes all dimmed with weeping, alas! without the poor little innocent adventurer, and nothing but the little wooden cross way up on the hillside amidst the pines to remind her of the hostage she had given to fortune.

All things come to those who wait—but there is no regular time-table.

The days got longer and the nights shorter, until the strange novelty of chronic daylight became a regular established institution.

In these latitudes, after the latter part of May, there is no such thing as darkness, which is a nuisance, and causes no end of complications. Unless a man keeps a diary and checks off each twelve hours as it is produced, he very soon loses track of the day of the week, which, although of no vital consequence, might enable him to distinguish between night and day, which would help him somewhat.

The day of the month is soon lost sight of, and not much required outside of civilization; but with the day of the week gone too, and nothing to fall back upon but the *year*, a properly brought up church member becomes discouraged and confused. He finds himself or herself having breakfast at ten o'clock at night, and innocently going to afternoon teas at five a.m. This would undoubtedly lead to confusion anywhere except in Alaska, where everything goes, even the night. It is at first most difficult to sleep when the sun is high in the heavens, and most annoying, after getting up, to find that everybody else has just gone to bed.

This climatic absurdity is responsible for wholesale hideous irregularity, which ends up by everyone doing just what they feel like. They eat when they are hungry and drink when they are dry, sleeping between meals if necessary. At last the hot sun and warm wind slowly but surely melts the ice in the lake, and it lazily moves off towards the Arctic.

All this time we have not been idle, and many a weary trip back to the summit has been made, ever bringing down supplies. My two Canadian canoes, four thousand miles from their home, looked well as they were launched from the ice into the first open water on Lake Lindermann.

LAKE LINDERMAN. AUTHOR AND ONE OF HIS MEN IN CANOE.

XII

EXHILARATION

JUNE the 1st, and a warm bright sunny day, the horrors of the Chilcoot behind us and almost forgotten, the last of the ice rushing frantically down to the Arctic Ocean, grinding along the moss-covered banks and scrunching past rocky cliffs, great floes of fast-rotting honeycombed ice reluctantly leaving their winter quarters and sailing majestically along, to be rent asunder with a terrible crash by the first rock encountered in the stream. Ice everywhere, ice to burn! sometimes piling high up on the banks, gigantic cakes of many acres forcing themselves on top of the smaller fry and leaving their mark away up on the bark of the spruce-trees, ever hustling northward to the mouth of the mighty Yukon, there to lie in wait and harass the early spring steamers, until dissolved by the scorching rays of an almost vertical sun.

A little miserable wheezy portable sawmill was puffing away day and night at the head of Lake Bennet, tearing spruce logs to pieces for one hundred dollars a thousand feet. Everybody was building a boat, lumber was hard to get, and, as each plank was worried off the log by the unsharpened screeching teeth of that wretched little circular saw, there were a score of applicants ready to take it away, and in ten minutes that plank was rapidly being transformed into some sort of craft.

YUKON RIVER. ICE BREAKING UP IN THE SPRING

One of the proprietors of this little gold mine, who also possessed an unpronounceable name, said to me, 'Spose I no gettee de logga, I no makee de lom.' He was a picturesque scoundrel, evidently of Irish extraction on the mother's side, and had given up washing since attaining his majority — he was not much over forty at this time.

There must have been about four hundred people, making four hundred different varieties of death-dealing conveyances. Once in a while you would see something resembling a boat, but not often. As a general rule, the soap box and coffin combination was the most popular pattern. Anything that would float was at a premium, and it was not an uncommon sight to see two men in an alleged boat jauntily leaving the head of Lake Bennett with all sails set in the morning, to be found quietly sinking the same afternoon.

Some men could not wait to be supplied by the mill, but went in for whip-sawing their own lumber. This is apparently an innocent and harmless amusement, but it leads to suicide or insanity. One man stands on top of the log and the other below, the saw is then pushed up and down along a chalk mark until the lower operator's lungs are filled with sawdust, when the work has to stop.

There was a story going the rounds of the different shipyards, that two 'pardners' commenced whip-sawing, when after working awhile the lower one excused himself for a moment, and, having hired the first man he met to take his place in the pit, disappeared. The sawing proceeded, until the uppermost 'pardner,' all unconscious that he was working with an entire stranger, bethought him of a similar device, and making some ordinary explanation climbed down and hired an Indian to do the sawing. The 'pardners' discovered each other shortly afterwards in an adjacent saloon.

My boat was designed in three minutes, and built, launched, and loaded in three days.

The motley mob, with its daily and hourly recruits, was becoming annoying and distinctly unsanitary. I determined to sail, although the pitch was barely cold in the seams of the boat. So, on a Sunday night, we loaded up the cargo, stowed anyhow, pitched things on board generally, and with five men and a dog we were under way at last with a fair breeze and a sense of freedom; with two thousand five hundred miles of waterway ahead of us, and a feeling of exhilaration and independence impossible to describe.

XIII

INUNDATION

It did not take long to discover that our tight little craft leaked like a sieve; in fact, we detected two feet of water lurking in the hold almost before the cargo was taken on board, and we had to submit to three 'jeers' from the assembled multitude on the beach as we alternately loaded in supplies and baled out water. Being, however, descended from a long line of proud and haughty ancestors, we persevered in the determination to make a start at all hazards, and kept a bright look-out for a good place to land, well out of sight of our late companions in misery.

The *Eva* was twenty-six feet long and seven feet wide. She was strongly built and very green. The planks upon which depended the lives of six good men and true, not to mention one absolutely useless dog, were but a few days before innocently growing in the wilderness, little dreaming that the ruthless axe of the wily woodsman would so soon nip the ambitious pine in the bud, transform him into a boat, and start him down the great waterway towards the land of gold.

It was humiliating certainly, with all sail set and a fair wind blowing, to be compelled to land as soon as possible, but as the water gained upon us there was nothing for it. So, selecting the first streak of sandy beach, I ran her up head on. Although ten p.m. it was still broad daylight, and we proceeded to unload the cargo. My ship's carpenter had neglected to caulk the bottom seam, which accounted for the leak. With the aid of a Spanish windlass, hastily rigged, and many cursory remarks, the little vessel was hauled up high and dry and the deficiency rectified.

Then came a wasted day and a foul wind; but next morning the prevailing southerly breeze came howling out of the pass again, and we were soon plunging down the centre of Lake Bennett, the staunch little *Eva*, in spite of her scow-like proportions, making short work of the twenty-one miles to Cariboo Crossing, on the three-mile river, which connects with Tahgish Lake.

It was a great relief to get away from the madding crowd—to escape, if only temporarily, from the filth of the huddled-up encampments and the chronic profanity—to once more breathe the pure air of heaven, and, forgetting all past miseries, to sail or drift contentedly down this mighty waterway.

Speaking of profanity, it seems to be indigenous to the Alaskan soil. It is particularly ornamental, and calmly permeates the most ordinary conversation, absolutely without any provocation whatever. It struck me that extremely original and elaborate able-bodied oaths were often completely thrown away upon trivial subjects, when they might have been kept on hand for a more worthy occasion.

I saw a lady struggling to put up a

small tent, which blew down as fast as she got it up, with persistent and no doubt irritating regularity. With the natural courtesy of my sex to females in distress, I detailed a man to go over and assist her. He soon fixed up the tent, and, being of a jocular disposition, suggested that when things went so contrarily it was a pity that she had not been born a man, so that she could swear. The lady replied, quite unconscious of any implied compliment,

'Why, mister, I'll be —— —— if I haven't cursed that —— —— —— —— tent the whole —— —— morning, but it didn't do a —— —— —— bit of good, by ——'

You could see the snow thaw round that tent.

I sometimes thought that driving dogs might be responsible for a good deal of the trouble—there is no doubt about its being infectious.

I have known dog-drivers who could make a golf-player blush.

XIV

EMANCIPATION

My little crew was now divided up into regular watches, as there was no reason why we should not run night and day. I decided, for the proper preservation of discipline, to adopt the usual sea regulations, where the captain stands no watch. There is no doubt I missed a good deal of sublime Arctic midnight scenery by this arrangement, and many a grand sunrise which alas! I can never recall, but the boys used to tell me all about it in the morning.

With everything snugly stowed under our half-decks fore and aft, one big white square sail bellying out before the south wind, the little cook's galley forward, consisting of a sheet-iron stove securely imbedded in a box of sand, the smoke from the slender stove-pipe streaming ahead, and without another living thing in sight, we felt emancipated. Two men slept, while four stayed awake to navigate the ship and admire the scenery.

On Tahgish Lake the wind, our only means of locomotion, decided to go back on us. It blew in fitful gusts or lulled entirely. We were often taken aback when we least expected it, then becalmed and made utterly helpless. Old Boreas had it all his own way in the narrow defiles of the Chilcoot Pass, and was much given to blowing about it; but here it seemed his force was spent, and he would try to sneak back to the blue Pacific Ocean.

A strange phenomenon occurs in this lake. About midway down on the right-hand side, the Windy Arm enters from an easterly direction. It is correctly named. Some of my people were out fishing in a canoe, and, noticing the big white caps running in this arm of the lake, came on board and reported that although we were entirely out of wind there was a large surplus over there and nobody seemed to be using it.

In less than an hour we had worked our little ship over to the east shore. Then with much toil, by poling, towing, pushing and shoving up this Windy Arm, having secured a substantial offing in order to avoid a group of rocky islands, we made sail, and with a big oar jammed down amidships as a leaboard we simply flew—the Jack pine mast, always unreliable, in which I had not the slightest confidence, bent like a fishing-rod with a twenty-pound salmon on. However, all's well that ends well, and that evening we tied up opposite Tahgish Houses, on the Six Mile River, a deserted Indian village, while the piscatorial artist of the outfit exhibited his skill and wasted his time in securing a few ill-conditioned grayling. These we condescended to devour at nine p.m., and then sailed with a fine fresh fair wind for the foot of Marsh Lake, about twenty miles.

XV

CONTINUATION

I CANNOT forget waking up on this particular morning when nearing the foot of Marsh Lake. The wind, which at first had been strong, got gradually weaker during the night, and when I relieved the watch at four a.m. it had died a natural death.

It was June 10th, and a close muggy atmosphere hung over the lake. A ghastly silence prevailed, with the exception of the merry buzz of the enthusiastic mosquito. This gentleman quickly notified us that he had come to stay and was ready to do business. McClintock Island loomed up on the starboard bow, and dead ahead lay the opening where the Lewes River commenced its downward career. But alas! the delay caused by waiting to ensnare a few wretched grayling was fatal. Another hour or less of that favourable breeze, and we would have been in the current and independent of any atmospheric disturbance. As it was, we had to pull wearily onward, providing an excellent breakfast for many hundreds of voracious mosquitoes, and arriving at last at the head of the Lewes or Fifty Mile River, as this part of it is called; when, with one man steering, the rest could go to breakfast and forget the horrors of the preceding night.

All day we drifted, rowed, and sailed, as opportunity demanded, an occasional thunder squall breaking the monotony—the river muddy, and the surrounding scenery uninteresting; until, late in the afternoon, the estimated distance being almost run out, a red flag on the bank told me we were approaching the celebrated Miles Cañon. The swift current became more swift, and soon the dark chasm, with its perpendicular basaltic walls, came in sight.

The superior sailing qualities of the *Eva* had enabled us to pass during the night four Scandinavians, who followed us closely all day. Evidently believing that we knew the river well, every time we hoisted our canvas, they ran up their sail; should we put out a sweep to help our boat past a dangerous point, out went an oar from their boat—in fact, they imitated

MILES CAÑON. LEWES RIVER

us to perfection, and arrived at the head of the cañon within five minutes of the time we landed.

XVI

HESITATION

There is a time in the tide of the affairs of man who go down to the Yukon in boats which taken at its flood leads on to destruction.

I had arrived at this point, and decided to camp and look over the situation.

I believe in taking ordinary precaution to preserve life, and I do not consider that men should be asked to incur extra hazardous risks without a generous equivalent; but on these waters the spirit of

MILES CAÑON, LOOKING DOWN STREAM

adventure becomes rampant, and everybody is in a hurry to get there at all costs.

One celebrated explorer, lecturer, and writer says:

'The White Horse Rapids are there, and may be run by those who are anxious to say they have done it;' but with the next breath he remarks, ' As for me, I am not anxious to say so.'

I tried hard to get some sort of an intelligent description of the much-dreaded ' White Horse,' but in vain. I met many men who had seen the monster, and many more who said they had. Some with a natural talent for lying, probably honestly inherited, and with descriptive powers no doubt cultivated, attempted to explain the difficulties and dangers of the situation. I used to get them to draw plans of the locality in the sand, which developed a good deal of hidden artistic talent, but failed most dismally to convey the slightest idea topographically to my bewildered brain. And now I was face to face with the real thing. Owing perhaps to native modesty and natural politeness with which I am afflicted, I did not assert my rights, which I might easily have done, insisting upon going through in the boat; but, after a careful examination of the cañon, I came to the conclusion that it was perfectly easy, and could be run with comparative safety *by the others.*

There were three men in a boat who were about to make the trip—a very young man, whose features were entirely concealed by an enormous arrangement of mosquito-netting, which gave him the appearance of an Egyptian mummy; a very venerable, grave, and reverend-looking seigneur with golden spectacles; while the third, who had evidently constituted himself master of the ceremonies, was a glib-tongued Yankee, whose total ignorance of the gravity of the situation gave him an air of confidence which evidently imposed upon the other two innocents. They had a frail-looking, sharp-nosed craft, of amateur construction, and before making a start the general manager of the expedition delivered a short oration. He said,

'Neaow, boys, there ain't the slightest particle of danger; look straight in front of you and watch me, don't be skeared, just pull your best.'

The wretched crew cowered behind their oars in abject fear and trembling. The younger man did not even remove the numerous folds of mosquito bar which entirely obstructed his vision and prevented him taking in the surrounding scenery, while the ancient one glared through his golden glasses, fascinated, snake-like, by the voice of the charmer.

With a sort of mangling movement on the part of these tender-feet, the boat was presently induced to leave the eddy and soon shot out into the middle of the stream, where we watched its fate from the rocks above. Just as they arrived at the first plunge, the well-meaning idiot in the stern frantically waved his paddle and yelled, 'Klondyke or bust;' then the paddle was swiftly whipped out of his hands and he fell flat on his nose in the bottom of the boat, while his pallid companions mechanically described circles in the air in an impotent manner, and thought hard of their past lives.

With no helm to guide her, the little craft plunged into the enormous rollers and turned completely round, then banged up against the rock wall of the cañon till she

MILES CANON. SCOW RUNNING DOWN

cracked, and only by the merciful interposition of Providence were the unfortunate occupants eventually picked up below in a thoroughly scared condition.

Miles Cañon is five-eighths of a mile in length, one hundred feet wide, and one hundred feet high. Through this gorge the whole force of the river is driven with alarming rapidity. The water in the centre is piled up four feet higher than that on the sides. Time, one minute, forty-five seconds.

With our mast unshipped, a close-reefed stove-pipe, and everything securely lashed down, our boat was run through the next morning flying,—our own artist getting a snap-shot at her from the rocks above.

Then came a mile and a half of very rough rapid water, thickly studded with rocks, any one of which was quite sufficient to upset the best calculations. But luck was with us, and we made this safely, towing the two canoes, which I had ordered to be carried over the cañon. Landing on the west bank, we thanked our stars and lunched.

The noblest Roman of them all, the fatal 'White Horse,' was still ahead of us and had to be examined. Another mile and a half of white caps playing leap-frog and chasing each other down to the final plunge, and the navigator knows his fate.

I took my steersman along and walked down to take a look at this picturesque spot. On the way there, a well-meaning old fossil, a fellow-voyager, shuffled out of his tent and implored me not to attempt the passage.

'Go and see for yourself,' said he, 'and then you will never try to run it. Only

LOOKING DOWN STREAM TOWARDS THE DREAD "WHITE HORSE"

[To face p. 89]

yesterday two poor fellows were drownded. You will see their boat on the rocks.'

I assured the old gentleman that we had no thought of suicide.

After looking over the situation carefully and consulting my pilot, we concluded to take the chances, although we discovered that no boat of our size had been down that spring. But I had two good and valid reasons: firstly, we had nearly six thousand pounds of stuff on board, which with so few men would take a week or more to pack down; secondly, it would be all over in two minutes one way or the other, and I really believe drowning is preferable to packing. Still, the sight of a good-sized boat split fore and aft lying on the rocks, and the dark and ominous warnings of the old croaker aforesaid, were very discouraging.

The 'White Horse' proper is a very

narrow part of the river, where the water fiercely boils and plunges through at a terrific rate. Big combers are forced up on the side of this whirlpool, and threaten to engulf the luckless craft that is not kept pretty straight and well-handled.

I tried putting a log through this chaos of waters, just to see what it would do, with most discouraging results. The log sailed gracefully through the centre, riding serenely over the heavy swells at about forty miles an hour, and, just as I had concluded it was all safe and easy, my log suddenly stood up straight on end, and, looking me in the face, plunged out of sight into some subterranean passage which was not laid down on the chart, disappearing for ever.

Of course, in the event of my boat tak-

THE DREAD "WHITE HORSE"

ing the same course, the public would have escaped the infliction of these pages.

At two p.m., the *Eva*, once more dismasted, and everything covered with tarpaulins, was cut loose, and at 2.02 or thereabouts she was safely moored below the much respected ' White Horse.'

It was soon over—a rapid run to the brink, a couple of plunges, a ton or so of water on deck, a blinding smother of foam—then congratulations and a horn of rum for all hands, including the cook.

XVII

ISOLATION

The four poor Scandinavian navigators who followed us so religiously to the head of the cañon came to grief on the sunken rocks in the swift water below, and when last we saw them they had a leaky boat and a puzzled expression in several different languages.

Our Jack of all trades was a man of vast and wonderful resource. He could make anything, and did not seem to require the raw material. I never saw his like.

He could make a fiddle, and play it too; a suit of clothes or a pair of boots were nothing to him. He was a veritable 'tinker, tailor, and candlestick maker' all rolled into one.

Besides this, he could build a boat and steer her anywhere in bad water. He was an excellent cook, an enthusiastic and successful fisherman, and an all-round first-class handy man.

This kind of man is bred only in the backwoods of Canada, and is invaluable outside of civilization, when at any moment an emergency may occur requiring absolute genius to overcome a difficulty.

This Jack of ours was garrulous, and invariably the hero of his own stories, generally 'chestnuts' of the most modern type. He was addicted to patent quack nostrums, from the old reliable Pain Killer down to the latest fad in pills, but particularly affected Electric Oil, which served him as a panacea for all conceivable ailments. He had a good stock of this stuff, and applied it upon the slightest provocation, externally and internally. It seemed to me to be equally efficacious for a headache or corns.

We carried an ordinary medicine chest containing the usual allopathic remedies, which, with the aid of a 'Sea Captain's Guide,' I used to dispense when necessary.

But there was one small bottle without a lable which always puzzled me. It contained a bright yellow concoction, with no directions. However, it fascinated our John, and, after sampling all the other horrors, he eventually concluded that the corner bottle was intended for some internal injury which he immediately proceeded to develop, soon devouring half the contents of this much-neglected remedy, and declaring himself cured by the first dose: it subsequently turned out to be a liniment for scalds.

John's peculiarities were numerous, but his good qualities and accomplishments were perfectly marvellous.

We were now drifting down the Lewes River to Lake Labarge, and, hearing there were large fish to be had, our John produced splendid troll, manufactured out of a tin can in ten minutes, with which he caught salmon trout from four to ten pounds in weight.

The little block at our topmast head was carried away, but what matter? With a sharp jack-knife, the invaluable John soon whittled out another one, through which our signal halyards worked as well as ever.

We were becalmed for two and a half days in Lake Labarge, which is thirty-one miles long and from five to ten miles wide, and quite capable of getting up an angry sea when the wind blows. I had to seek the seclusion of a little rocky harbour on one occasion when a strong contrary wind arose, and we lay there all one day, in company with two other boats that had been driven in for shelter.

After leaving Lake Labarge, the current in the river is decidedly swift for thirty-two miles, and there are many rocks to be avoided, if possible; but the water is beautifully clear and the bottom of the river distinctly visible all the way to the mouth of the Hootalinqua River—a good-sized stream, said to be navigable for steamers of the flat-bottomed variety all the way to its head waters, Teslin Lake.

SLEIGHING BOATS ON LAKE LA BARGE

Steering a boat from Lake Labarge down this thirty-two miles is, to say the least, quite interesting—hard-a-starboard one minute, and hard-a-port the next, with many a big jagged black rock to arrest your further progress suddenly if you do not move quickly.

My boat was strongly built of two-inch plank throughout, with several pairs of natural knees which we cut out of the woods at Lake Bennett, and plenty of seven-inch spikes.

In the event of striking a rock, I wanted to hurt the rock most. In many places the current is running fully eight miles an hour; and taking an average of several hundred miles by the chart, I found it to be 5.75 miles per hour. This is fast enough for anybody, especially for those folks going the other way.

The geologist of the party, who was

H

given to deep mental abstraction and invariably wore a confused expression, requested to be put on shore, murmuring gently some unintelligible remark about the pre-Adamite glacial period. Our John took this as a personal insult, believing it was a reflection upon his cooking: he had attempted pancakes that morning for breakfast.

The geologist wandered aimlessly along the shore and disappeared round a point, while the rest of us, not understanding the first principles of geology, simply sawed wood. After several hours had passed, a search party was detailed in one of the canoes to go and discover the scientist or bring in the mangled remains for identification. Breathlessly I awaited the return of the canoe, fearing the worst, knowing full well the success of the expedition depended largely upon the recovery of the learned geologist.

The sun was shining brightly and the air was balmy. A large flat rock, picturesquely situated on the river edge, was warm, and no doubt seemed to suggest the correctness of the ancient glacial theory. A faint snore from this locality indicated the presence of the missing savant, who had fallen asleep while struggling with the great problems of nature.

There were some unkind enough to remark that he had escaped cutting wood.

On another occasion, our only botanist, anxious to secure specimens of the fauna of the country, started out with a repeating rifle, and, after an absence of many hours, returned empty-handed, with nothing but the positive assertion that there were no cariboo to be found and nothing to be seen but a measly brown bear who was too thin to kill.

XVIII

OCCUPATION

THERE is a certain fascination and a blissful feeling of independence in drifting down a large river with a swift current. The ever-changing panorama prevents monotony; and the discomfort of six men in a boat with a large dog, always in everybody's way and particularly at meals, is soon forgotten. Our sleeping accommodation was not of the best, and sometimes it was dangerous to attempt it. There were occasions when a tired mariner, attempting to snatch the proverbial forty winks, would be rudely awakened by somebody walking on his face. Sometimes exhausted nature refused to stand it any longer, and, huddled up in the after-part of the boat, out of the way of the helmsman, or stretched out face downwards on our little forward half deck, we would fall asleep in relays; when that much-dreaded sharp rasping sound, denoting that we were being swept swiftly over a bar, soon dispelled our dreams of home and happiness, and made us sit up and think. Then, in crooked reaches of the river, we would have to put out an oar on either side to avoid being carried against rocky points or swept into false channels. Mile after mile, night and day, we drifted, rowed, or sailed down this great water-way, north, always north, onward to the golden goal.

The 'Five-Fingers Rapids' was a very tame affair after the 'White Horse,' and was soon negotiated. I went ashore to take a look at this piece of water, and was received by a most bloodthirsty deputation headed by a band, which drove me back to the boat and the conclusion that death from drowning was preferable to being eaten alive. So I did not examine the water.

Many people who have travelled through unsettled countries have died in the firm belief that they have seen mosquitoes, but unless they have visited the Yukon this is a mistake. It was reported to me that we should probably meet cariboo, moose, bear, etc., but the mosquito was the only wild animal encountered. He is of the sandy-haired, long-legged variety, with a Roman nose and a voracious appetite. The family were originally vegetarians, until they were converted by the arrival of the oriental tender-foot, which they now prefer to any other dish.

After the 1st of June they are met in herds, and attack on sight without provocation.

XIX

PALPITATION

On the tenth day after leaving Lake Bennet, at eight o'clock in the morning, we sighted Fort Selkirk, the old historical ruins of a Hudson's Bay post, at the junction of the Lewes and Pelly Rivers. A register kept here by the present storekeeper showed that seven hundred and thirty-six people had passed down this spring, and one hundred and thirty had been seen who did not register.

A pause of a couple of hours was all

we could afford; a few purchases of tobacco and other luxuries, and we were off again on our watery highway, the veritable Yukon River at last in all its muddy glory, and over four hundred miles from our sailing-point.

Another hundred miles found us at the mouth of the Stewart River, which being at its flood poured into the Yukon at a terrific rate, increasing its already swollen appearance.

A few miles below the Stewart a boat was sighted containing five men, who were wearily tracking up stream, pulling, pushing, and shoving, hanging on to the perpendicular walls of the cliffs, and working like demons. They did not take long to tell us their secret. A new discovery on Henderson Creek—only a few more miles, and they would be there. Gold had been discovered only a few days

MINERS ON THE WAY DOWN IN THE SPRING [*To face p. 107*

before, sixty-five claims had been staked already, and three hundred men were coming up over the mountains from Dawson. 'Why not turn back?' It sounded tempting. Meanwhile we were drifting past them at the rate of eight miles an hour, and the idea did not seem feasible. Besides which, these stampedes were of daily occurrence, and generally resulted in much hard work and disappointment. I listened as they shouted the news, and drifted on in search of some corroboration of their report.

That afternoon we made the Sixty-Mile post, a small store with nothing in it, situated on an island, and here they told us again of the wonderful new discovery. A man named Henderson had located the discovery claim a few days before, and of course ' there was millions in it.'

I had very little experience of these stampedes, although I got quite used to them afterwards. But it seemed like flying in the face of Providence not take advantage of the golden opportunity; so I hastily fitted out a canoe with a couple of weeks' provisions, and despatched two men to the scene of the recent find, with instructions to locate two of the richest claims immediately, while I would proceed in the morning to the much-longed-for Dawson City.

XX

DISSIPATION

At 4.30 p.m. on the 18th of June, forty-one days from Dyea, estimated distance five hundred and seventy-five miles, the valley of the Klondyke hove in sight. A long line of boats, all sizes and shapes, strung along the river front, told us that we were at our journey's end and that Dawson City was reached at last.

A perpetually frozen muskeg is the foundation which will support the proposed Dawson City. At this time the

'City' consisted of several hundred tents straggled along in the mud for about a mile and a half. There were a few dance-houses and saloons, also a saw-mill, picturesquely situated in about the centre of the main street. The two rival trading companies were rushing up stores and warehouses; and the utmost confusion, combined with the most villainous odour, prevailed.

In the midst of mud, refuse, roots, bushes and filth of all kinds, there was a swearing, sweating mob of reeking humanity—gamblers, whisky men, and adventurers of every description, an occasional old-time miner, the usual sprinkling of women, Indians, and the omnipresent dog.

As the various specimens of the genus 'tender-foot' arrived in the midst of this charming community, they would plaintively enquire where the best place was to look for gold.

The saloons were running night and day. Almost every device for gambling was in full blast, and nobody seemed to take the least interest in anybody else. The worst kind of American whisky could be obtained for fifty cents a drink. Everything was paid for in dust: there was no other currency, and a large cautionary sign was displayed in all the gambling-rooms,—'Don't overplay your sack.' Gold dust representing tens of thousands of dollars was thrown about as if it was so much oatmeal, and it was no uncommon sight to see a couple of thousand dollars staked upon the turn of a card.

Withal there was very little drunkenness, and lawlessness was a thing unknown.

At night the dance-houses were always well patronized, and the charge for indulg ing in the mazy waltz with the fair but frail patronesses was only one dollar, of which the lady received twenty-five per cent. The old-time miner is usually anxious to distinguish himself by dancing as often as possible; but when there was a large crowd the ladies were compelled to distribute their favours equally, and were never monopolized for more than one dance by the same partner—quite an innovation on the methods in more civilized society.

Outside the busy buzz of the only saw-mill, running night and day, mingled with the tramp of many feet churning up the black muck, made confusion worse confounded; while the intolerable perpetual daylight made everything seem reversed, and gave the poor pilgrim an unutterable longing for home and civilization.

The possessor of a good claim turning

DAWSON CITY FROM OPPOSITE BANK OF YUKON RIVER [*To face p. 113*]

out five thousand dollars a day could no doubt put up with this sort of existence and possibly almost enjoy it; but a man with human instincts had but one desire, and that was to get away as far and as fast as possible.

XXI

PRIVATION

I soon discovered that Dawson City was not the sort of place to select for a residence, and decided upon a temporary suburban retreat.

Half a mile below the Metropolis I discovered a spring of sparkling cold water, and just enough flat country to accommodate a tent ten by ten; here I fetched up.

Two hundred and forty hours without having had your clothes off makes you

AUTHOR'S CAMP BELOW DAWSON CITY

feel like really going to bed. The thick matting of moss was inviting—the softest couch we had seen since leaving the Driard House, Victoria, two months before; and at eleven o'clock that night, with the sun shining brightly, I succumbed to nature's sweet restorer. But alas! immediately below the mossy cushion the hard blue ice soon made its presence felt, producing a cold moisture which sent an icy chill through the spinal column and disturbed the slumbers of the weariest.

Imagine, if you can, a country perpetually frozen and carefully carpeted with moss a foot or more in thickness, so that the sun's vertical rays, however strong during the short summer, could never hope to penetrate. A mighty river bank full, always rushing towards the Arctic, whose muddy waters were unfit to drink—a scarcity of almost the bare necessities of life, and a population devoid of one congenial soul to swap ideas with.

The utter loneliness and unattractiveness of this desolate gloomy wilderness can never be properly described, and the hopelessness of accomplishing any useful object became daily more apparent. Two steamers belonging to the two great trading corporations were alongside the bank, and they were the only means we had of sending to the outer world the news of our safe arrival.

There was no post-office and no postage stamps, and we were at the mercy of the courtesy and the honesty of the steamboat pursers. I figured that my letters probably went to San Francisco before they could be mailed: eighteen hundred miles down the Yukon to St. Michael's, three thousand two hundred miles to San Francisco, and about three thousand miles across the

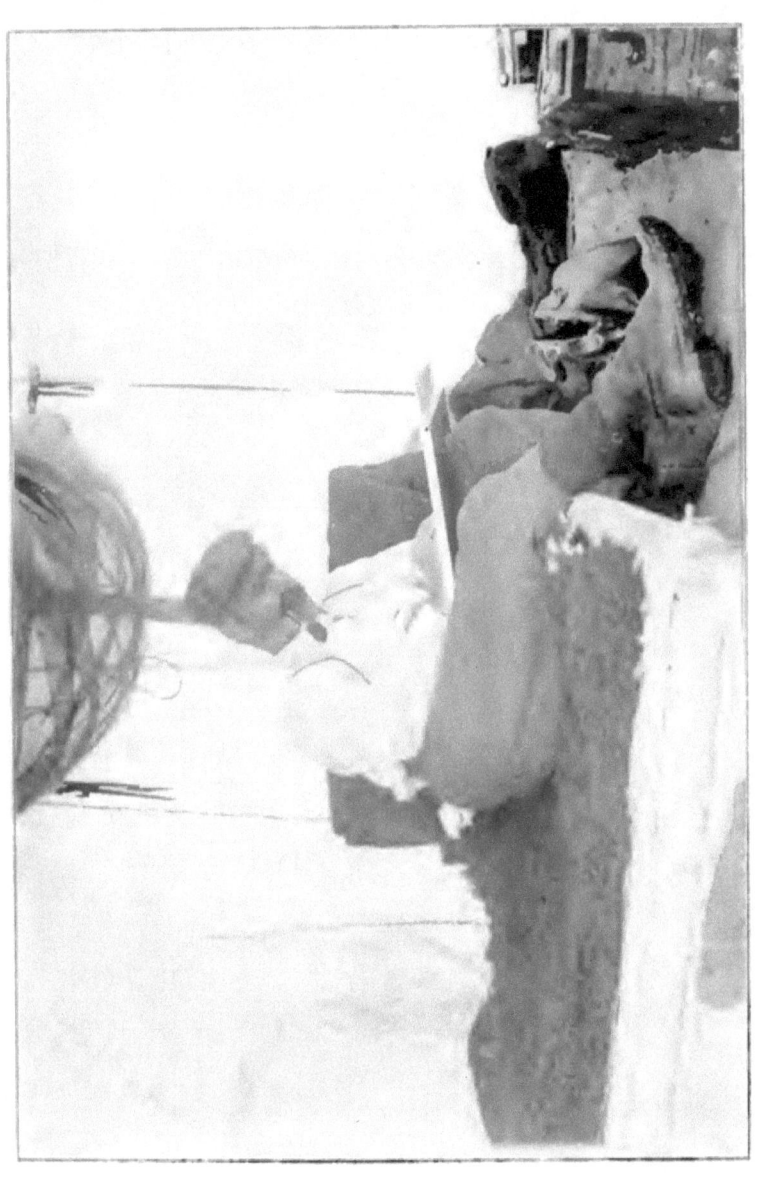

INTERIOR OF TENT. AUTHOR WRITING DESPATCHES

continent to Canada: only a matter of eight thousand miles. This melancholy but accurate calculation made me feel homesick.

Provisions at Dawson City were very scarce, and, although not actually on short rations, we had to depend entirely upon the supplies we had brought in. The first boat connecting with the ocean ships was not expected till July, her arrival depending principally upon the movement of the ice-floes at the mouth of the river.

The creeks tributary to the Klondyke River were all located, and there were no other accessible places to prospect, even if prospecting had been practicable; which, as a matter of fact, it is not during the summer, as the surface water prevents the prospector from reaching bed-rock, and, as this is the spot it is necessary to strike, very little prospecting is attempted during the summer season.

The thermometer stood at ninety six in what it was pleased to call the shade, and yet venerable blue ice could be found six inches under the moss. Millions of voracious mosquitoes came to board with us, and soon the aggravating though invisible Yukon gnat made his unwelcome appearance. The Henderson Creek stampede returned with a report that it was a 'fake'; my two prospectors, having abandoned their canoe, had wearily tramped up the creek many miles, with pack on their backs, to find nothing, and were finally driven out by bush fires, which made it altogether too hot even for them.

Out of a hundred men who located claims on this creek, only *one* thought it worth while recording; and yet some day, when prospecting is made easier and transportation facilities are improved, this

AUTHOR'S CABIN. "THE BEAR'S DEN."

much-abused creek may perhaps turn out rich.

I concluded, while waiting for further supplies and developments, to provide my little crew with exercise by building a cabin, and, having discovered about one hundred trees in the immediate vicinity, large enough for house-logs, we commenced operations.

How we did work! Trees had to be *felled*, as men say in England, and rolled or pulled down to the site of the cabin, while all the time the merry mosquito was making himself unpopular and disturbing the calculations of the architect.

The day's work over, it was the correct thing to go uptown and see what was going on; but there is a certain sameness about drinking and gambling which eventually becomes monotonously expensive and fails to produce any excitement.

I generally preferred solitude, and seldom left the camp.

About the only excitement I had worth recording was a terrific thunder-storm. Up in these latitudes the lightning seems to be more vivid and the thunder louder and more of it. The wind blew a hurricane and shifted all round the compass many times during the night, the trees round the camp were bent like whips, and the water in the river was lashed into foam. The rain came down in torrents, and made matters more interesting by loosening some rocks on the mountain-side, which came roaring down behind the camp.

This was about the break-up of the summer, or at any rate the hot weather, which, I figured, lasted thirty days. It went out with fireworks, and ended in a bank!

A few days after this violent storm, while I was sitting alone, building castles in the air and writing letters home which I knew I could never post, a crackling in the bush announced the arrival of a stranger. He was a typical prospector, a big, good-looking, good-natured giant, a regular Gabriel Conroy. After bidding me good-evening and enquiring if I was the boss, he proceeded to unbosom himself at once.

'Pardner, you ain't afraid of ghosts, be yer?'

As it is considered *infra dig.* in that country to acknowledge being afraid of anything, I assured him that I was the proud possessor of unlimited courage, and had more nerve than I could conveniently pack.

'Well,' said he, 'pardner, I've brought a dead man down here, got him in a boat.

I've tied him up under them bushes. You won't mind if I leave him there for a while, will yer?'

I assured him that any friend of his was most welcome, dead or alive, but ventured to suggest that, as the weather was still warm, perhaps a funeral might be advisable.

'Oh, you needn't be the least mite skeered. He'll keep all right. Why, he's guaranteed for thirty days.'

And then he told me the particulars of the tragedy. The deceased and my visitor were, as he remarked, 'sort of side-partners,' and were prospecting away up the Eldorado gulch. On the night of the big storm they were sleeping together under a sort of makeshift tent, when a tree was blown down and killed the young man instantly, smashing in his skull. There was no one else near, and, after cutting away the top of the tree and discovering that his 'side-partner' had done with prospecting in this world for ever, my friend started off in search of help, and they actually packed the body twenty-five miles on their backs down to Dawson.

'I had him in the company's warehouse,' he said, simply, 'till yesterday, but the captain told me I had to take him away, and the *or*-thorities won't allow me to keep him in town.'

I again suggested a funeral, when Gabriel looked serious and explained his reason for delaying the final operation.

It seemed that the dead man had a brother, who was prospecting away up another gulch, and he had been sent for, as they thought it was only right that he should be the chief mourner. So they decided to keep the late-lamented above ground till the arrival of his brother. With this end in view, they had, with the aid of a tin-smith and many soldering-irons, managed to can the unfortunate victim in a sort of home-made casket, so that he would keep.

And there he lay in the bottom of the boat, covered with a heap of pine-boughs, moored to the bank,—a quiet, well-behaved, and, at present, inoffensive neighbour.

'Good-night, pardner,' said Gabriel; and then, looking over his shoulder, 'Keep an eye on him, will yer? Yer see, the boys might take it into their heads to play a josh on me, and come down and cut the line and let him go.'

But they did not, and every morning Gabe would come down to take a look at his silent friend, till at last, after about a week, he came one day and proudly announced the brother had arrived, and the funeral was ordered for two o'clock that afternoon.

The ordinary miner dearly loves a funeral. To him it is an event not to be neglected. It is announced by crude notices posted on trees in conspicuous places, and the solemnity of the occasion is highly appreciated and most impressive. The virtues of the deceased are generally discussed, and his many good qualities often exaggerated.

The last day that Gabriel arrived to announce the funeral arrangements, he presented me with a formal invitation to be present at the obsequies, which, however, I was unable to accept. He then made the suggestion that I should send a couple of men in canoes to follow the boat containing the corpse, remarking with pathetic innocence and tears in his big blue eyes, 'I think, boss, that would make a nice little *per*cession-like, and give him a decent sort of send-off, don't you?'

The natural born prospector, *i.e.*, the genuine article, is the most hopeful and the most confident creature in the universe: failure to him simply whets his appetite—success merely encourages him to seek fresh fields—the most appalling obstacles rather increase his desire to penetrate the inaccessible and possibly discover the hiding-place of the precious metal.

Inured to hardships all his life, and anticipating nothing better, he religiously pursues the undulating vagaries of his adopted calling, without a murmur.

Theories born of long experience are constantly exploded, which makes no difference to him: he patiently plods along, working hard to discover the great secrets of nature, living a hard life, and often dying a hard death, 'unwept, unhonoured, and unsung.'

Once I asked Gabriel how it was that, having prospected all over the continent, he had never become rich. He quickly assured me that once he discovered a mine in Colorado, and sold her for forty-seven thousand dollars cash. I naturally wondered why he did not keep this amount and retire; to which he replied,

' Wall, boss, I jest tell yer how it is with us prospectors. The time I sold thet mine and got all thet money, I thought I was a big son of a gun, but I wanted to be a —— —— *great big son of a gun*; so I took thet money, and blowed it all in on a quartz lode in Idaho which warn't worth a cuss: so I lose the whole pile.'

The last I saw of him, he was working for wages on Bonanza Creek, trying to secure a 'grub-stake,' which meant another excursion into the interior.

XXII

EMIGRATION

The most feverish excitement prevailed now in Dawson. Stampedes to various improbable creeks were of hourly occurrence, and I have seen a long line of men with fifty-pound packs on their backs cautiously sneaking off at midnight to climb the hills on a wild-goose chase.

I knew one poor little plump attorney from some backwoods American hamlet, who followed a stampede for nearly fifty miles, rigged out in a long-tailed black coat, paper collar, and the thinnest of thin boots, over hills and through swamps, gradually but surely getting behind, till he met the vanguard returning unsuccessful and discouraged, also well fly-bitten. The lawyer turned back, perfectly well satisfied with his experience.

At last, on the 25th of July, the long-looked-for steamboat arrived, twenty-one days out from St. Michael's, the first messenger from the sea and the outside world. She had one hundred passengers and some real potatoes.

The fleet on the Yukon River at this time consisted of the *Portus B. Weare*, *J. J. Healy* and *C. J. Hamilton*, belonging to the North American Transportation Company, while the Alaska Commercial Company owned the *Alice*, *Billa*, and

Marguerite — all flat-bottomed, stern-wheelers, and with a totally inadequte capacity to supply the multitude daily arriving at Dawson City. They seldom made more than two round trips in a season, and sometimes only one. Their cargoes were not always selected with a view to relieving the pangs of the hungry miners: in fact, I heard of one vessel said to be loaded with whisky and billiard balls, not a very nourishing sort of diet. However, time changes most things, and I believe both companies have since built several new steamers; besides which, there will be innumerable others, belonging to private concerns and English trading companies.

Having paid a flying visit to the richest of the now celebrated gulches, I decided to emigrate by the first returning steamer.

Bonanza Creek is most disappointing from an artistic point of view. A small, brown-coloured stream meandering through a narrow valley of muskeg, the hills on either side covered with a stunted growth of spruce, it certainly did not seem a very inviting place to look for gold. But, twenty or thirty feet beneath this frozen black muck, millions of dollars have been calmly resting on the bed-rock for countless ages. It struck me that gold was always hidden in the most remote and impossible places, no doubt to prevent its discovery; but this Klondyke gold went one better, and, not content with being in an almost inaccessible country, after burying itself in the most unlikely-looking ground, it arranged for a perpetual frost. And yet, in spite of all these difficulties, it has been discovered, washed and dressed, then trotted

RICH DIGGINGS ON BONANZA CREEK

[To face p. 132

off to the San Francisco mint, to be transformed into those great big beautiful shining eagles.

XXIII

EMBARKATION

On the evening of the 26th of July, having said farewell to my late companions in misery, I went on board the steamer *Portus B. Weare*, and, as we steamed away amidst the plaudits of the assembled multitude, I felt that I had at last taken a step in the right direction. True, there were one thousand eight hundred long watery miles to be traversed before we reached St. Michael's, with a hazy possibility of finding a ship there to transport

NIGHT ON THE YUKON. END OF THE RUN

us two thousand four hundred miles to some civilised port. But what matter? We were once more bound for the outside world, for the land of newspapers, railroads, and telegraphs, where we could exchange ideas with civilised nations and get something decent to eat and drink.

I had not accomplished the original object of the expedition, which had turned out to be impracticable; still I had succeeded in securing interests in some good claims, and left my men to look after them during the long Arctic winter.

The *Portus B. Weare* was not the most comfortable boat in the world, and she carried many more passengers than she could possibly accommodate; but we were bound home and could put up with anything for six or seven days, which is the ordinary duration of a passage.

I remember the first night out. Having secured an upper berth, I was only just comfortably asleep when the whole concern came down with a crash on top of two returning miners, wounding one of them and nearly scaring the life out of the other. I picked myself up out of the *débris*, and subsequently slept on the floor. We found in the morning that the berth was of a very flimsy construction, and we had to rebuild it.

Fort Cudahy, or Forty Mile, was passed early that night. The place was absolutely deserted. And the following night we arrived at Circle City, which was also pretty well depopulated.

Precisely at midnight, some thirty miles below Circle City, we struck on a sand-bar. This was the 27th of July.

XXIV

INDIGNATION

THE Yukon River, where it runs through what is called the flats, is supposed to be thirty miles wide for a distance of about one hundred and fifty miles; and this is where we were stranded.

The Transportation Companies are entirely dependent upon Indian pilots, natives of different sections of the river: it takes a good many of these gentlemen to pilot a boat down the whole length thereof.

The emancipated Indian pilot, with his hair cut short and a pair of high-heeled boots on his feet, is one of the most contemptible creatures imaginable. Presuming upon his superior local knowledge, he looks proudly down from his elevated pilot-house position and despises his white employer, for whom he has a thorough contempt. White pilots being unobtainable, this aboriginal abomination is generally petted and pampered until he is almost unendurable. He is the laurel-crowned hero of his own particular wigwam, wears the best clothes to be had for money, deserts the boat when he feels inclined, or piles her up high and dry for amusement at the dictates of his own sweet wayward fancy.

We had at the wheel a lovely specimen of this educated idiot, who was responsible for our disaster, detention, and destruction.

The *Portus B. Weare* was not a passenger boat; it was ill fitted, inadequately manned, and poorly provisioned. As the facetious were wont to observe, 'of the Portus Beware.'

About seventy-five souls, consisting of men, women, and even little children, were on board, and destined to remain, stranded in two feet of water—the prospect far from inviting. The old experienced Yukoner, accustomed to reverses of every kind, took it philosophically; while others of us, who had business elsewhere, chafed and fretted as the hours passed by without any hope of the boat getting off.

I remember the indignation of many passengers when the first eighteen hours had passed and we were still immovable.

It was fortunate we could not see into the future and know that we had to remain on that awful boat for eighteen long weary days and nights.

The usual passage for these boats down stream is about six days, and, as they do not provide against accidents of this sort, we soon experienced what it was to be short of provisions. The menu was not elaborate when we started, and after being out fourteen days it was soon reduced.

The waiters in the alleged saloon were the ungroomed children of the forest, a careless, happy lot, who threw plates at themselves and the passengers, chattered continuously, and tumbled over each other in their wild haste to bring you what you did not want.

The weather was hot, and the unfiltered water unfit to drink. We became like caged wild beasts, walking up and down and simply glaring at each other, sometimes stopping to curse the company for its bad management.

The captain, a little wooden-headed Scandinavian, tried several devices to spar the boat off, but only succeeded in getting her further *on* the bar; and all this time the water was slowly but surely falling, till, after breaking all the tackle we had, the Indian crew were formed into a shovel brigade and proceeded to dig the boat out.

There were about forty of them, and I often used to lean over the rail and watch the dusky warriors digging up a teaspoonful of sand to one gallon of water. They would stand in a long line, knee-deep in water, always chattering to each other, and when one paused to light his pipe all the rest promptly stopped.

Having nothing better to do, I made a close mathematical calculation that, at the rate these copper-coloured loafers were going, it would take them seven years, four months, nine days, two hours, and thirty-six minutes to dig a canal sufficiently deep to float the boat. A further calculation showed that, given two months' time to excavate the vessel by the same methods, so that we might get away before navigation closed, it would require 389,734 aborigines to accomplish the work in that time.

This seemed very appalling at first, and I feared there might be some mistake; but I carefully checked over the figures, and found them correct.

I thought it my duty to tell the captain about this, but he said if the river rose about two feet it would knock all my calculations endways.

We had now been so long on this gravel bar that we had a sort of residential, resigned expression of countenance. We seemed to feel that we belonged there, and were very jealous of our rights. In discussing the dangers of navigation, one pessimistic individual advanced the theory that any other steamer passing through that channel would likely strike on our bar. This idea was fiercely resented. We were there first, and we would like to see the steamboat that could take any of our bar from us. Little babies that were carried on board by their mothers could now be seen walking about the decks alone; and elderly men began picking out green spots on the shore for cemetery purposes.

We were utterly helpless, and could only wait for assistance to arrive from somewhere.

Our ship's boat used to go off for wood every day, and the engines were often kept turning to stir up the sand, so that we would not settle down there too permanently.

One night we discovered that eight or ten of our Indian crew had deserted, having surreptitiously made a raft while on shore and sneaked off down stream towards Fort Yukon. This seemed like the rats deserting a sinking ship, and was most discouraging.

At last our anxiety was relieved by frantic cries of 'Steamboat!' and a long line of black smoke down stream soon told us that the *Healy* was on her way up; and in a couple of hours she was abreast of us, tied up on the opposite

STEAMER JOHN J. HEALY, YUKON RIVER

bank. Our excitement and joy was intense, but very short-lived. After answering our signals of distress and holding a confidential conference with the authorities on board our stranded ship, the *Healy's* lifeboat shoved off, and shortly afterwards the steamer slowly steamed off towards Circle City. I find in my diary this short remark :

' Sent a fresh captain and some rotten eggs, then proceeded at nine p.m. Wish it had been reversed.'

The excitement was all over. We beseeched them to unload the *Healy* and take us down to St. Michael's, but all in vain. One valiant sportsman intimidated the little president of this big corporation (who was on board), and demanded the return of his passage money and a free pass back to Dawson, which was given him.

There was a great deal of indignation and a strong feeling against the company for getting us into this scrape and making no effort to get us out of it. We knew now that we must miss the ocean ship. The *Healy* had to go up to Dawson City and return,—another week at least.

This was most trying, but had to be endured. Our wretched boat was getting to be most unsanitary; the food was poor and abominably served; the weather was hot, and we were all more or less consumed with a feeling of having been duped, especially after paying one hundred and fifty dollars passage money.

The digging brigade was still operating daily. The new captain, a long lean son of the South, who invariably wore gum boots and a sour expression, had the reputation of having dug out more boats on the Missouri than any other man in the world. The middle-aged passengers regretted that they could not hope to see him dig out this one.

XXV

JUBILATION

At last, at midday on the 13th of August, the man with the field-glass made out the *J. J. Healy* coming down. No one believed him, as he was always seeing things, and the pessimistic passenger remarked ' that it was impossible for the *Healy* to return in that time; and even if it should be a steamboat, it wouldn't be the *Healy*; furthermore,' he remarked, ' that even if it was the *Healy*, he wouldn't mind venturing a trifle that she would never get here.'

Meanwhile, the smoke grew plainer. We climbed to the roof of the pilot-house, and soon recognized the well-known double smoke stacks, and in another half hour we received her with a sullen roar of satisfaction.

There was an intense feeling of relief, and everybody excitedly packed up, ready to abandon the wretched old water waggon that had been our home for so many uncomfortable days.

The kodak fiend took a farewell snap at her as we pulled away, and we were soon on board the *Healy*, and, if not moving, at least *afloat* once more.

Something wrong with the machinery detained us another day; but on Sunday, the 16th, we actually got away, and once more swept majestically round the bend into the swift current, at not less than fifteen miles an hour.

How good it seemed to be moving again, and on board a fairly comfortable boat, compared to what we had endured!

The days were now getting much shorter, and we were compelled to tie up every night. Our captain was a cautious man, and took no chances. He kept the lead going continuously in suspicious-looking water, and visited every wood pile in the country for fear of running out of fuel.

The lower Yukon is not an interesting river. It is plentifully besprinkled with missions and missionaries of every known persuasion. I do not believe there is room for another missionary of any kind. The otherwise neglected inhabitants submit patiently to the comforting consolations of the Church, with an occasional square meal, and it does not seem to do them as much harm as one might expect. There are Greeks, Russians, Roman Catholics,

Presbyterians, Episcopalians, Methodists, and Congregationalists for the benighted children of nature to chose from. The crops may fail, and it may be a poor year for hunting, but he is never stuck for spiritual advice.

So much competition for the privilege of saving his soul undoubtedly puzzles the aborigine occasionally, and he must find it difficult to select a religion.

There are so many ways indulged in by religious people of doing good, particularly in the Old Country. I saw a very handsomely embroidered altar-cloth, evidently constructed by the hands of some fair English enthusiast; when I saw it, it was being utilized as a breech-cloth by an old gentleman with a most murderously forbidding countenance.

The names of most of the places we put into were generally unpronounceable.

If you pronounced them as they were spelt, you would be sure to be wrong; and you could not possibly spell them as they were pronounced.

The delta of this great waterway down which we have been coming for nearly twenty-four hundred miles is said to be one hundred miles wide. There are many channels, and the spot where we tied up for the night when we reached tide-water was without exception the most dreary, desolate-looking waste I ever had the honour to gaze upon—miles upon miles of mud-flats, no vegetation, fog and drizzle; outside, the faint moaning of the waves in Behring Sea, making the whole scene positively funereal.

XXVI

COMMUNICATION

It is about eighty miles from the mouth of the Yukon to the Island of St. Michael's, and it is not a pleasant passage to make in a river-boat, with forty-five feet of her sticking up in the air and three feet in the water. I should not care for it as a steady job. When she commences to roll, if there is any sea on, and the upper-works begin to shift in an unpleasant manner, it is time to make other arrangements. The hull is the most inviting spot; it might possibly float. I kept one eye on the hold, which was unoccupied, and loafed round the main-hatch, waiting for the upper-works to go overboard; but, although there was a good deal of groaning and creaking, nothing happened, and we got into shelter behind St. Michael's Island that night. Only eighteen miles round to St. Michael's Harbour, but we dared not put our nose round the corner. There was quite a sea running.

The Indians here are a wonderful sea-going race, both men and women. They start with the tusk of a walrus, which they make into an ivory harpoon, to kill a seal. The skin of the seal furnishes them with a kyak, a small skin canoe, and in this wonderful construction they go out to sea and chase more seals and walruses, which provide them with more death-dealing ivory appliances, and more skins for boats, besides which they eat the flesh and use the oil for fuel, light, and drink.

They are very clever at making models of themselves and their boats, which they sell to inquisitive tourists and globe-trotters who chance to pass that way.

Their appearance is not very prepossessing, although, strange to say, all the women I saw on St. Michael's Island had splendid complexions.

They utilize every part of the seal, even making fine waterproof coats out of the intestines.

After a couple of days' more delay, which was a matter of no consequence now, the opposition boat, belonging to the Alaska Commercial Company, heaving in sight, we pulled out for St. Michael's Harbour, where, after some blood-curdling groans and screeches from the upper-works of the *J. J. Healy*, we arrived safely—just thirty days out, instead of six.

St. Michael's showed evidences of the gold excitement, there being no fewer than nine vessels in the harbour, four of them being steamers.

XXVII

CIVILIZATION

THERE were several ships to choose from, good, bad, and indifferent, bound for ports on the Pacific Coast; and I determined to take the first, which happened to be a wooden steam schooner called the *Excelsior*, bound for San Francisco: not that I wanted to go there, but rather on the principle of any port in a storm.

This vessel was chartered by the Alaska Commercial Company, and in many ways a comfortable little tub she was, always reminding me of Nansen's celebrated *Fram*, from his description.

Nansen's work was my only literature on the entire trip, and I devoured this religiously whenever I got the opportunity, until I knew it almost by heart.

The *Excelsior* sailed at midnight on August 26th, with ninety passengers and twelve boxes of bullion, worth probably in the neighbourhood of three hundred thousand dollars.

We steamed out into the Behring Sea, and all went well till next morning. I was on deck at seven a.m., and could not help noticing the muddy colour of the sea, denoting shoal water, although we were certainly sixty miles off the land. In a moment we were stuck fast on a mud-bank, in twelve feet of water, while we required fourteen feet astern to float.

I subsequently heard that this was not

an unusual occurrence. Opposite the entrance to the Yukon River an enormous shoal extends for nearly a hundred miles, and any ship trying to take a short cut is liable to stick. Some of the passengers had been with me in the unfortunate *P. B. Weare*, and, upon coming on deck and finding the ship stationary, took it all as a matter of course and part of the regular programme. But here we had an element of danger, as the Behring Sea is often disposed to be stormy, and, should a heavy blow come on before we got off, the ship might possibly break up and bring all our troubles to an untimely end.

The weather luckily was fine; and after working the engines several hours, in the hope of dredging out a passage, we succeeded in striking a sunken log or a rock, and broke three blades off the propeller.

Here was another unique position,—a disabled ship, fifty or sixty miles off the land, high and dry on a mud-bank.

At last the captain broke the news to us that, if we ever wished to get off, it would be necessary for the passengers to turn to and work. We had seventy-five tons of coal stored somewhere aft, and this would have to be shifted forward, when he expected the ship would float.

We soon divided up into watches and religiously moved this coal forward, using wheelbarrows, till a few minutes before midnight the welcome sound that we were afloat once more was heard, and we ceased from our labour.

But alas, our mutilated propeller was like a hand with all the fingers gone— nothing left but a thumb. With this abreviated appliance we had to make our way for eight hundred miles to Unalaska, the nearest port, in the Aleutian Islands.

Thanks to a favourable breeze and a fairly smooth sea, we accomplished this, arriving on the night of September 1st—thankful it was no worse.

The Aleutian Islands at this time of the year look very much like the coast of Ireland at first sight, until you discover volcanic formation—the hills are a bright green, and not a tree or shrub to be seen. Picturesque little harbours are plentiful, and, with a few sealing schooners and an occasional man-of-war anchored here, the effect is quite magical.

Our broken propeller had to be unshipped, and a second-hand one, which luckily we had on board, substituted,—quite a performance when far away from dry-docks and other conveniences. The ship had to be backed up on the beach at high water, and then, when the tide fell sufficiently, the business end could be extracted.

All this was skilfully attended to by the chief engineer, and in five days we were ready for sea again.

There was literally nothing to do except catch fish and watch the sea-lions disporting themselves in Dutch Harbour. H.M.S. *Pheasant* was the only representative of the English navy here, and, as the well-known bugle-calls came floating over the water in the evenings, many of us felt that we were indeed once more almost on the threshold of civilization.

We now heard for the first time of the loss of the *Mexico*, the ship which I came up in from Victoria to Juneau, and also that the *Eliza Anderson* had gone down with one hundred and twenty people a few days before we arrived. This ancient side-wheel steamer, built away back in the fifties, it appeared, had been sunk for many years, but, on account of the gold rush, had been resuscitated and chartered by some enterprising Transportation Company, to convey the uninitiated to St. Michael's for two hundred dollars per head.

The report of her loss, however, turned out to be incorrect, as the day before we left I saw her slowly steam into Dutch Harbour, looking very lopsided but still in the ring. The poor miserable passengers were very full of their awful experiences. They were twenty-eight days out from Seattle, cooped up in this wretched old tank, the vanguard of an irregular procession of many other ancient hulks. A few days before making this port, they reported encountering a storm which lasted three days and nights. They were entirely out of fuel, and had to burn parts of the wood-work of the ship. Many barrels of oil were thrown overboard to calm the troubled sea, and one very intelligent passenger assured me that when a big sea struck the ship, the seams would open and the water dash through the aperture across the deck. The same man informed me that the only way they were saved from a watery grave was the novel method of navigation adopted by their captain. This gentleman, realising the necessity of preventing, if possible, one of those big Pacific rollers from breaking over the vessel, would run her up to the top of a big wave, back astern, then go ahead again, thereby going up and down on the same wave for several days, until the storm was over. Having secured some few tons of coal from a deserted cannery somewhere along the coast, they at last made Unalaska, a thankful but thoroughly scared lot of Argonauts.

The ship was condemned, I believe, by the United States authorities, at the passengers' request; and these misguided people chartered a small sailing schooner to take them on to St. Michael's, paying fifteen hundred dollars for the luxury.

The stampede for the Yukon River had undoubtedly now fairly commenced, and any old box that would float was being pressed into the service.

About this time the steamer *Humboldt*, a brand-new boat, came in on her way down to Seattle and San Francisco, and I determined to transfer. I had already paid two fares, but did not hesitate to pay one more in order to expedite matters.

For the information of future emigrants, I may state that I paid the North American Trading and Transportation Company one hundred and fifty dollars, for which modest sum I was supposed to be entitled to a first-class passage to Seattle via St. Michael's, making close connection with a good ocean steamer. However, all I succeeded in getting was a residence for nearly three weeks on a sand bar, a charming resort for those having plenty of time to spare: then thirteen days more on another river boat. I then sacrificed the balance of my passage money and disgorged one hundred and twenty dollars more to the Alaska Commercial Company, which entitled me to a passage on the *Excelsior*—and a good long one too, it seemed to me.

The *Humboldt* had only about sixteen returning passengers, and was 'flying light.' She was a good boat, and capable of fifteen knots an hour; but, as coal was scarce, her speed was kept down to eleven and half, which would bring us to Seattle, bar further accidents, in six days and a half.

I gave up seventy-five dollars more for this chance of reaching civilization. This vessel had been chartered by an enterprising legal gentleman with an eye to the almighty dollar, who, for the modest sum of three hundred dollars each, guaranteed to deliver people at Dawson City, and easily secured over two hundred victims. I was told he took up a river boat in sections, and calculated to put this together at St. Michael's, and then, although supremely ignorant of the difficulties of navigating the Yukon River, he intended going up to Dawson before the ice made.

We had two of his passengers returning in the *Humboldt*, and they told me that when they left St. Michael's the others were looking for a convenient tree on which to hang the promoter of the enterprise; but, as there are no such things to be found on that volcanic isle, let us presume he is still safe.

It was dreary on board the *Humboldt*, but every day brought us nearer to the much-longed-for goal; and at last, on Sunday night, September 12th, we sighted the well-known light off Cape Flattery, at the entrance to Juan de Fuca Straits. I had often passed this spot before in a very matter-of-course kind of way, but this time it was the most welcome sight I had seen for many a long weary moon. We gazed at the lighthouse, through a thin veil of fog, long and lovingly, while visions of real porterhouse steaks, fresh green vegetables, clean shirts, newspapers, and other luxuries, rushed through our excited brains. As we steamed up the calm waters of the Straits, our hearts beat joyfully with a newborn hope, and all our troubles seemed to be ended.

A quiet, restful night, and next morning we were alongside the busy wharf at Seattle—once more in the midst of civilization.

APPENDIX

ALTHOUGH this narrative ends with my return to civilization, it is perhaps due to those of my readers who thirst for information, and may think I have treated the subject in too frivolous a manner, that I should provide them with a few statistics which they could only obtain through the medium of the numerous guide-books (trustworthy and otherwise) which have so recently deluged the literary market.

I have carefully avoided giving advice to enthusiastic Argonauts, neither have I intentionally discredited the country which has apparently absorbed the attention of the whole universe. I have simply endeavoured to relate my own personal experiences, and paint the peculiarities of people met with, during a trip of about thirteen thousand miles.

I cannot do better than quote from Mr. Ogilvie's latest report, as regards the necessary food supplies which the intending prospector will require. A table of approximate distances, taken from a leading Canadian daily paper, will also assist the stranger in the choice of a route; while the latest authentic Government mining regulations, although always subject to revision, will explain themselves.

It is generally expected that many thousand human beings, of all sorts and conditions, will form a vast procession and attempt to reach the gold-fields this year. Many have undoubtedly started without having had the opportunity of buying this valuable work, and therefore cannot be blamed ; but to the others, if there are any left, I would say remember Mr. Punch's advice ' To those about to marry.'

HINTS TO PROSPECTORS

FROM MR. W. OGILVIE'S REPORT

FOOD SUPPLIES, ETC.

For the information of those who have never been in the country I give some notes on the amount of provisions required, first stating that you will require at least fifty per cent. more in that region than you would in a more southern latitude. The cold suffered (often intense) for at least seven months in the year conduces to a vigorous appetite. This is a provision of nature, for, in order to keep warm, the human system has to pile on fuel just as much as any other apparatus where heat is required.

All supplies required for the Yukon by persons going in on the Pacific side can be obtained at the cities of Victoria or Vancouver. The merchants at these places have had many years' experience in outfitting miners and prospectors, and know exactly what a man should take with him, according to the conditions under which he is going to travel or work, and know from many years' testing, and from the experience of northern explorers who frequent the British Columbia cities, what class of goods are most desirable and useful, and those best calculated to complete a traveller's outfit. Many things that are excellent for more southern districts, and which are sometimes sold to inexperienced explorers, are not fitted for the more northern districts of what was once Hudson Bay Company's territory.

The merchants of these coast cities have studied and are thoroughly familiar with the requirements of the country, for many parts of which, including the Kootenay, Cassiar mines, and other districts, they have outfitted exploring parties for many years past. By purchasing in either of those two cities for the Pacific journey, a considerable percentage of cost is saved in freight duties, etc. The Canadian customs duties on goods purchased out of the Dominion range from twenty-five to thirty per cent. alone, so that aside from the question of paying freight on extra baggage, it is obvious that a considerable saving is made by purchasing necessary outfit in Canada and at the nearest point to the Yukon territory where such supplies can be procured.

Those who go into the mountains or into the Yukon from the east side of the Rocky Mountains, across the plains via Calgary and Edmonton, will find the same conditions to apply. The merchants at the principal points have had a wide experience in outfitting people for the mountains. During the past season many have chosen this route, and purchased necessary supplies at Calgary and Edmonton, at both of which towns there are large outfitting establishments. As between the two cities of Calgary and Edmonton a traveller can choose for himself. The cost of the several articles he will require will probably be found, freight included, to be about the same. It will be well to remember, therefore, that it is better that Yukon outfits should be purchased at Victoria or Vancouver, if the purchaser is going in on the Pacific side, and at Calgary or Edmonton, or other Canadian point, if he is proceeding by the plains route. The articles that should be taken are:

Of flour we require at least four hundred and fifty pounds for a year's consumption. This should be of fairly good grade. It need not necessarily be fine flour, but should be good medium. Oatmeal or rolled oats, fifty pounds; cornmeal, twenty-five pounds. This latter I do not consider so necessary as oatmeal, as oatmeal is a warming food. Bacon (good, fat), two hundred and fifty pounds; hams, fifty pounds; evaporated dried apples, twenty-five pounds; dried peaches, twenty-five pounds; and if you have a fancy for any other kind of dried fruits you can take them along, or substitute them for one or other of the above. Good black tea, twenty-five pounds. In that country you will find a cup of good, hot, black tea, after a long, cold tramp, very invigorating—in fact, it proves 'the cup that cheers but not inebriates.' Coffee, ten pounds; sugar (good granulated), one hundred pounds. If you take the ordinary brown sugar in the winter it freezes into a hard lump, and is very difficult to manipulate. Not so with granulated; remaining dry, of course it remains powdered. Beans, one hundred and twenty pounds. There are several kinds of beans of which you may make choice according to your taste, but the ordinary bean sold there is the brown bean, about twice the size of the small white one. Pot barley, ten pounds; rice, fifteen pounds; extract of beef, two dozen four-ounce tins. I have found Johnson's Fluid Beef to be very good. Baking powder, twelve or fifteen pounds; **salt, thirty pounds; pepper, one pound**; mustard, one pound; compressed vegetables, ten or twelve pounds, depending upon the kind you take. Canned fruits may or may not be taken, but they are bulky and heavy, consequently inconvenient, and in winter a source of trouble in that country, as the contents freeze solid and require a very long time to thaw. You should also take ten or fifteen or more pounds of baking-soda, as you may think necessary.

In case of scurvy one might provide limejuice, more or less as their taste suggests, but the dried fruits already named are antiscorbutic in their action, and if we wish to make further provision in that direction we might take two or three dozen tins of good orange marmalade, and a similar quantity of strawberry or raspberry jam. These, as put up by some firms, are very good. Dried potatoes are put up in several forms, and are good. Twenty-five or thirty pounds of these should be taken. Other vegetables are put up also, from which you may select as you fancy, but you should take the above quantity of potatoes, and eight or ten pounds of dried onions. Take along also a few dozen yeast-cakes, you may have a chance to use them once in awhile, and their weight and cost are trifling. For convenience, I recapitulate, in list form:

	Pounds.
Flour	450
Oatmeal	50
Cornmeal	25
Bacon (good, fat)	250
Hams	50
Evaporated dried apples	25
Dried peaches	25
Tea	25
Coffee	10
Sugar	100
Beans	120
Barley (pot)	10
Rice	15
Extract of beef, say	6
Baking powder	12
Salt	30
Pepper	1
Mustard	1
Compressed vegetables	12
Canned fruits, say	30
Jams in tins, 1 pound each	24
Baking soda	10
Potatoes and onions	35
Total weight	1,316

This will prove ample to spare for any healthy, vigorous man, work as hard as he may, but it is well to have a little too much rather than too little. It is well also to bear in mind that there is much waste connected with the ordinary transport and use of provisions under the conditions generally attending prospecting, and the cooking incidental to it.

It will be noticed that the above list contains no canned meats. These are sometimes convenient when making a journey, and their use is largely a matter of taste. Some relish them, while others have 'no use' for them. In this line, as in some other matters, each will consult his own taste and means. Packed in tins as they are, they are somewhat inconvenient to pack, and the tin adds considerably to the weight. For preservation it is absolutely necessary that the stuff be hermetically sealed. It is a pity some more convenient mode of putting up were not adopted, lessening the weight, while not risking spoiling by contact with the air.

APPENDIX

The cost of this outfit will, of course, vary considerably, according to time and place of purchase, but in any of the cities or towns where you are likely to purchase all your requirements will likely cost no more than two hundred dollars, and may be less. At the prices ruling on the Yukon it will be more than double that; four hundred and fifty dollars is rated as a fair 'grub stake,' that is, your requirement for one year.

The following list and prices are furnished by an Edmonton firm, subject, of course, to fluctuations in the ruling prices elsewhere, which will not, however, affect the gross amount very much. Taken as a whole the amount will not differ much from the same list at other points:

	Dols. cts
4 sacks flour, 98 pounds each	10 00
20 pounds corn meal	70
40 pounds rolled oats	1 30
25 pounds Indian rice	1 75
100 pounds beans	4 50
Carried forward	18 25

HINTS TO PROSPECTORS

	Dols.	cts.
Brought forward	18	25
75 pounds granulated sugar	4	87
75 pounds evaporated apricots, peaches, and apples	10	25
6 packages yeast cakes		50
20 pounds candles	3	00
150 pounds bacon	16	50
25 pounds butter	3	75
10 pounds baking powder	2	50
3 packages soda		30
20 pounds salt		40
1 pound pepper		25
Half-pound mustard		25
Half-pound ground ginger		25
10 packages evaporated vegetables	2	00
2 dozen condensed milk	4	50
10 pounds tea	4	00
25 pounds coffee	10	00
Half-dozen Abbey's effervescent salt	3	60
Laundry soap	1	00
Matches		80
Evaporated potatoes and onions	4	00
2 pairs heavy blankets	14	00
2 suits underwear	5	00
2 cottonade shirts	1	50
2 sweaters	3	00
Carried forward	114	47

APPENDIX

	Dols. cts.
Brought forward	114 47
1 heavy suit	7 50
1 pair pants	2 00
1 pair overalls	1 25
1 mackinaw suit	10 00
2 pairs arctic sox	1 50
6 pairs wool sox	1 50
2 pairs mitts	1 00
2 pairs moccasins	3 00
3 towels	75
1 pair rubber boots, hip	5 00
1 pair laced boots, miner's	5 00
Mosquito net	50
Buttons, needles, and thread	25
1 camp cook stove	5 00
1 gold pan	75
1 knife and fork	15
2 spoons	5
1 large granite spoon	15
1 large fork	10
1 granite cup	15
1 granite plate	15
1 whet stone	10
1 pick and handle	1 25
1 hatchet and handle	75
1 axe and handle	1 25
Carried forward	163 57

HINTS TO PROSPECTORS

	Dols. cts.
Brought forward	163 57
1 whip saw	9 00
1 X cut saw	3 50
1 hand saw	1 00
1 long hand shovel	1 00
20 pounds nails	1 00
2 files	40
1 draw knife	75
1 plane	90
Brace and bits	2 00
3 chisels	75
1 butcher knife	25
1 compass	50
Rope	1 50
1 fry pan	25
1 hammer	50
1 auger	65
1 bake kettle	1 50
1 best copper kettle	6 00
1 steel pail	75
1 granite wash basin	40
1 candle lantern	35
1 pound quicksilver	90
1 pair goggles	35
1 caulking iron	75
10 pounds pitch	1 00
Carried forward	199 52

	Dols.	cts.
Brought forward	199	52
15 pounds oakum	2	00
Sundries	2	18
Total	203	70

A few words on packing, or putting up the goods for transport, may be of use to many. Flour should be put in a good cotton sack, fifty pounds in a sack; two of those are then put into a good strong gunny sack. For ordinary transport this is not more than enough, and for prospecting tours one of the fifty pound sacks inside the gunny sack will be found quite sufficient. Sugar, beans, rice, barley meal, and bacon may be packed in the same way, with advantage.

I would not recommend oiled cotton for covering, the oiling seems to rot the cotton fibre and render it easily torn, besides in cold weather it is as brittle as glass, and the result is we have no covering at all in a few days.

The gunny cloth, if good and heavy, will

exclude quite a lot of rain. In the case of flour a thin layer of it will get wet and form a dough which excludes water almost perfectly; that amount of flour is, of course, lost, but that is provided for in the amount above given. In wet weather sugar will have to be carefully looked after, as once wet the action seems to continue until the whole is converted into syrup if the temperature permits, and if it does not it is frozen into a mass as hard as rock. These remarks may be in a good degree applied to salt, and I would say emphatically look after your sugar and salt. Compressed tea offers the advantage of less bulk, and if it is not taken, get tea put up in pound tins as some of it used to be. This is convenient in use, as only a small quantity of it is opened at one time, and we obviate deterioration of a large amount of it through exposure.

The other articles may be packed in cases for transport into the country, and then put up to suit convenience. Care should be exercised that none of the cases weigh much over one hundred pounds, until we have better transport facilities than at present exist. That is about all the ordinary untrained man wants to handle, and for some months to come there will be much manual labour in connection with transport there.

Bedding and other things of that kind one will have to provide as suits his peculiar needs.

In the way of clothing, the principal difference between that country and this is, that one requires much heavier underclothing. The ordinary woollen garments, such as worn by lumbermen and others in this climate, are sufficiently heavy for that, except when travelling on the open or on the rivers, in which case some sort of fur is necessary, more especially if it is blowing. Ordinary woollen coats will not keep out the winds, and when the thermometer is forty or fifty degrees below zero, and a twenty to thirty mile wind blowing, one is not very long exposed before considerable suffering ensues. Good heavy woollen mitts, with a pair of deerskin mitts over them, is all that is required.

In the way of bedding a good heavy fur blanket is almost indispensable; ordinary woollen blankets, no matter how many one has, will not keep warm. But in this there is a wide latitude, depending on differences of physical constitution. I have seen two men in the same tent at the same time with the same amount of bedding, one sleepless from cold and the other comfortable; hence, as I said before, each will have to determine for himself as suits his temperament. Of course the less one can do with the more convenient it is.

Blankets have been made in that country of fox, lynx, wolf, and bearskin. They are very expensive, costing from sixty to one hundred and twenty dollars, depending upon the nature of the fur and the size of the blanket. In the future, however, they are absolutely out of the question, for the supply of fur there is constantly diminishing, and it is only a question of a year or two until none will be found in the vicinity of the diggings, nor anywhere near them. These should be procured, if possible, here. Lynx makes a very durable, light, warm blanket, and I would recommend it above all others, on account of its lightness and warmth. Fox is good, but not so durable as lynx. Wolf is also good, but heavier, and not so warm as lynx, and the same may be said of bearskin.

I have no doubt that necessity will induce manufacturers to devise some cheap substitute for fur. Sleeping-bags are made which will be useful and comfortable. Of these I would say choose the one that gives you the most thickness between you and the ground, of course not neglecting the covering. Often in winter, when camping out, more cold is felt from below than above. Waterproof clothing is not suitable for that country in the winter. The intense frosts so harden it that it cracks, and soon breaks into pieces. A good, large

DOG TEAM, YUKON RIVER

[*To face p.* 193]

raccoon skin overcoat is very desirable. It is cheap and durable.

While travelling in cold winter weather your knees will give you more trouble than any other part of the body. I have found a fur covering for them, resembling a section of the leg of pants, about one foot long, and fastened to your under-garment so as to cover the knee, is all that is required. Whatever material is used it should be wind-proof and thick.

The other things that one may require will have to suggest themselves to each one for himself, but too much need not be taken. Do not load yourself down with extras. Rubber boots are indispensable during the spring, summer, and autumn months. These can be procured in the country at from ten to fourteen dollars per pair—that is, miners' boots, which come up the full length of the leg. Shorter ones cost less, of course. These may be taken as they can be procured cheaper, but there is nearly always a good assortment on hand at the trading points.

In the way of hardware one requires a couple of good chopping-axes. Axes are sold with a double bit—that is, a double-edged axe of which one may be kept in fair order for chopping, and the other used for rougher work. A brace and set of bits is indispensable, ranging from a quarter to one and a half inches in size. Hammer and wire nails, different sizes, are also indispensable; the more you can take of these the better, but, of course, the quantity will have to be regulated by your transport facilities. A small hand-saw is absolutely necessary, with an assortment of screw nails of different sizes, and suitable screw-drivers, and an inch or one and a quarter inch auger will prove very useful. A miner's pick is also indispensable, and a miner's shovel. Of rope we require twenty-five or thirty pounds of assorted sizes, from one-quarter inch up to one inch, and if we contemplate building a boat for ourselves, a whip-saw, oakum, and pitch. Of the latter, ten to twenty pounds may be taken, and five to ten of the oakum. The other articles of hardware, such as dishes, knives, forks, spoons, kettles, etc., each one will have to select for himself. His supply should be based on his prospecting intentions and the length of time he expects to be absent from points of trade.

A rifle and a shot-gun may prove useful and are a sort of necessity, but as a rule they prove of very little use, as game is seldom met with, and what little there is, one has no time to follow. Hunting is an art which requires long experience to develop. Occasionally one obtains a shot at a moose or cariboo, but these are often accidental, and your gun may be carried for years without benefiting you one dollar. Still, by all means take them along. You may require them, you never know when, and when you do require them you require them in earnest. Fishing-hooks and lines may be taken, but of these it may be said as of the guns.

Needles, thread, and yarn and cloth, for mending and patching, are required, of course, and each one will have to determine for himself the amount he needs. You cannot make a mistake by taking more than you actually contemplate using, as the weight and bulk is unimportant. A small medicine chest is imperative. For contents of this I would suggest medical advice. What would suit one, another would not require, and each will have to determine for himself and for his peculiar case just what he should take. Paper, envelopes, pens, ink, and pencils are necessary, as you should never neglect to write whenever possible; by all means keep up the connection with home. If you can procure powders for making ink take them, as most of the inks sold are injured by frost, besides the liability to break your bottle when it does freeze.

A pocket compass is useful, and if you take one take a good one, with a needle not less than an inch and a half to two inches in length; and when selecting, take the needle which takes the longest time to settle after being put oscillating. The one which settles quickly is useless. It may be stated generally that the magnetic needle points east of true north from thirty-two and a half degrees at Lake Lindermann to thirty-six at the boundary.

In moving about the country a boat is absolutely necessary. There are no regular lines of steamers on the main river at present, though possibly there may be in the coming season; and if there are, they will only take us along the main stream from one of the minor streams to another, as we may desire. Landed at the mouth of a small stream, we require some sort of a boat to make progress in.

Now boats made there are necessarily heavy and imperfect in construction, also of bad form. I would advise taking some light, easily portable boat from here or elsewhere, as one may procure it easiest and best. In my opinion the best boat for general use in that country is of the canoe form, many of which are built in the Province of Ontario and elsewhere. The pattern I would suggest is commonly known as the Peterborough, or Rice Lake canoe, of which many kinds are made. Bass wood is the best wood for all round use. I give the dimensions of some of them.

A seventeen foot canoe, forty-one inches wide and seventeen inches deep, will weigh about one hundred and thirty or one hundred and forty pounds when dry. This canoe will carry twelve or fourteen hundredweight, and two or three men. Of course this will load it pretty well, and if our load is bulky it requires some experience to stow it away in a boat of that size. Practice soon overcomes this.

An eighteen foot canoe, forty-three inches wide and eighteen inches deep, will weigh a little more, and carry a hundred or two hundred more pounds easily.

A nineteen foot canoe, forty-six or forty-seven inches wide and eighteen inches deep, will weigh when dry about one hundred and seventy-five or one hundred and eighty pounds, and will easily and safely carry eighteen or twenty hundredweight and two or three men. Larger ones are made, of which I give some figures:

Length	Width	Depth	Weight	Capacity	Price
21 ft.	49 ins.	18 ins.	135 lbs.	2,200 lbs.	51 to 57 dols.
22 ,,	50 ,,	18 ,,	140 ,,	2,500 ,,	54 to 60 ,,
23 ,,	51 ,,	18 ,,	145 ,,	2,700 ,,	57 to 63 ,,
24 ,,	52 ,,	18 ,,	150 ,,	2,900 ,,	60 to 66 ,,

Another make:

Length	Width	Depth	Weight	Capacity	Price
23 ,,	50 ,,	24 ,,	275 ,,	2,850, 12 in. draft 5,120, 20 ,,	58 ,,
25 ,,	50 ,,	24 ,,	300 ,,	3,200, 12 ,, 5,600, 20 ,,	60 ,,
30 ,,	50 ,,	24 ,,	350 ,,	3,800, 12 ,, 6,500, 20 ,,	75 ,,

The above weights were furnished me by the makers. The weights in the paragraphs preceding the list are from my own observation, after the canoe had been used awhile. In actual use the water the wood absorbs will increase it ten to twenty pounds.

The freight rates on those canoes, from where they are made in Ontario to Vancouver, is about two dollars sixty-five cents per one hundred pounds space weight, with a minimum weight charge of eight hundred pounds; or, in other words, you are charged for the space the boat occupies. Now, by nesting them—that is, taking several of the different sizes, the smaller ones inside the larger ones, say a twenty-two foot, twenty-one foot, nineteen foot, and eighteen foot—space weight, crate and all, about the limit—eight hundred pounds—costs twenty-one dollars twenty cents, or about five dollars thirty cents each. If you wish to pay for actual weight the charge is about ten dollars fifty cents per hundred pounds. Nesting is by far the best way to send them, and large parties going can have their canoes put up that way with lessened risk in transport, and less cost than if sent singly. This I would advise to be done.

In ordering a canoe, order with an eighteen or nineteen foot canoe five or six good, specially heavy paddles, not less than five feet nine inches long. If any of the makers manufacture poles for poling, I would advise those to be taken along too. They should be made of good, straight-grained white ash or other light, strong wood, from eight to ten feet in length, about one and half inches thick at the lower end or point, tapering to about one and a quarter or one and an eighth at the top, on which a round knob should be left, say one and a half inches in diameter. The point should have a socket steel point put on over the wood and fastened to it with a screw, so as to be easily taken off. These will prove convenient on our journeys for other uses than poling, and much more durable and handy than any we may get in the country.

Also procure a canvas cover of sufficient size to cover the canoe completely, so made that it can be fastened down when necessary and prevent wind blowing it away. This may be ordered from the makers with advantage, they having the benefit of their own and others' experience. It will prove very useful, and often save us unloading our boat during a rainy period.

Down stream in one of these boats is easy work. In making our way up stream we have to resort generally to poling or tracking, as the current is generally too swift to be surmounted by paddling. Poles can be got in the country, but if they can be procured at the makers, as above stated, by all means take them. Unless they are iron-shod they soon what is called 'brush' at the point, that is, the soft wood bruises and gets brushy. This has to be cut off from time to time, and the pole is soon reduced in length by this constant wearing. By all means get them iron pointed, or steel is still better. Several kinds of points are made, but a good blacksmith will easily and quickly turn out a half-dozen or more socket points, to be fastened on with a screw or nail at very little expense; and any kind, so long as it covers the end of the pole, and is capable of being securely fastened to it, is good enough.

In poling the boat or canoe, the poler stands up, puts the end of his pole to the bottom and shoves on it, the man in the stern steering the canoe as may be desired, while still shoving. To the uninitiated this is a very difficult and laborious work, but a little practice soon gets one into the knack of it, and it is wonderful how a boat can be propelled by two or three men who are accustomed to this work. As much as thirty or thirty-five miles per day has been done, but the unaccustomed would probably tire themselves out in one-third of that.

Where the water is deep—that is, more than three feet, which is a fair depth,—or where the bottom is too soft for poling, as in mud the pole sinks into it and is difficult to withdraw, (in fact, the withdrawal often nullifies the effect of the push, and the boat stands still, and the beach is suitable for walking on,) we resort to tracking,—that is, a small, strong line is attached to the side of the boat some three to six feet from the bow; another line, called a bridle, is fastened to the bow and to the hauling line four or more feet forward from where it is attached to the boat. If this line is properly attached, the boat will steer itself. The hauling line being attached to the side of the boat tends to draw the bow out so that she will run across stream, but the bridle counteracts this, and with proper adjustment the result is that the boat follows along a few feet out from the shore. It requires very little attention from the man steering,—in fact, the only attention he bestows on it is to see that it avoids rocks, trees, and other obstacles along the beach, and in rounding points he has to manipulate the boat to keep her away from the point.

This is by far the easier mode of taking a boat up stream. Two men hauling on a line on a fair beach will walk from two and a half to three miles per hour, if they so desire, and haul the boat up bad places with comparative ease. I have seen a boat taken up a pretty steep rapids in this way at a good smart rate. After the pair on the line have kept up this gait for half-an-hour or an hour they become warm and somewhat tired. With a party of four the two in the boat change places with those on the line, taking a similar spell, as it is called, and those on the line take their places in the boat. When the last two become tired and warm they take a spell in the boat again, and so on.

Thus, between hauling and resting, they can keep up a good smart gait without fatiguing themselves very much. Four lively, good men, along a fair beach, will generally be able to haul a boat or canoe, such as I have described, twenty-five or thirty miles per day, and at the end not feel nearly so fatigued as paddling or poling would make them. A greater number, of course, will have an easier time, and less a harder time, but two men can do a good day's work in this way. Myself and a man have made twenty-four miles up stream in a day in this way, and made a survey while doing it.

The line should be light and very strong. To haul an eighteen or nineteen foot canoe of forty-five or forty-eight inch beam, with ten or twelve hundredweight and two men, the line should not be more than one-eighth of an inch in thickness. Of course, its quality should be first-class. There are lines made which suit this purpose admirably, known as cod-lines. I cannot give the numbers of the various sizes, but simply say a line one-eighth of an inch thick is sufficient to haul a boat of that size with a load anywhere that a boat can be taken.

Of course, a heavier boat requires a somewhat heavier line, but I have seen boats forty to forty-five feet long and nine feet beam, loaded with eight or ten tons, drawing two feet of water, hauled up strong currents by a line not more than one-fourth of an inch in thickness. The objection to a heavier line is that its weight sags it, and unless the current is very strong it is continually sinking into the water, which increases its weight. This renders it liable to catch on sticks, tree-tops, rocks, or other things which are generally found plentifully strewn along the river banks. The men on shore will soon acquire the knack of flinging the line over any obstacle of that kind, providing it is not too heavy. A sharp, upward jerk will hoist it feet above anything we desire to avoid, if given at the right time. To do this the bow of the canoe should be turned across current, just before the line is thrown up. This holds the canoe out against the effect of the pull on the line. Often a high tree-top or other obstacle can be passed easily by turning the boat out into the current; this runs her up and out, so that if the obstacle is close to shore it is passed without any attention from the men hauling.

Care should be taken when the boat is running up in an eddy below a point, with a swift current rushing past it, to enter the boat or canoe into the current as nearly as possible bow on, and not across the current; by entering this way into the current gradually, no time is lost and no risk is run. I have known several boats to be swamped by running them up the eddy as far as possible, and suddenly turning them into the swift current; the result being the water boiled over the side of the boat and filled her. Had the men given way on the hauling line in time this would not have happened, or had the line parted as a light line would have done, all would have been well.

I call particular attention to this and its attendant risks. A little practice will soon enable one to do this. Take plenty of line for that purpose, but do not take it too heavy. As a rule, not less than sixty feet of line should be out, even under the best conditions, and in rough water, or along a bad shore, more is required. Not less than one hundred and twenty feet should be ready for use when required, so fastened that whenever required it can be let out quickly and free from knots and twists. There are several ways of doing this. One is to have the line wound around a reel or bit of board at the front end, which the hauling man can pay out as he deems necessary, and wind in again when he sees fit. Cotton line is unsuitable. The water has a bad effect on it. It soon cuts and rots, and is not so strong as good jute line.

TENTS.

Of course each one has his own idea of a tent, but experience has taught me that the simpler the tent is in construction the better. I would suggest a bell tent not less than ten feet in diameter, with a ten ounce duck roof, and an eight ounce duck wall. The wall to be two and a half or three feet in height, with a foot or more of sod cloth. The pitch of the tent should be pretty sharp, to throw off the rain. I would not have it less than nine or ten feet in height. Better than this, a square tent, called the 'Egyptian' tent, ten feet on each side, with a ten ounce roof and eight ounce wall, as in the bell tent. Of course a smaller tent may be ordered, but this will prove a good serviceable size, and will not be too heavy to pack around, and will accommodate three or four men conveniently. The square, or Egyptian tent will accommodate four men and quite an amount of outfit. One man can hoist one of these tents readily by driving in four stakes in the form of a square at the proper distance apart, fastening four of his guy lines on them, inserting his pole, and raising the tent. Afterwards he can adjust the other guy lines and fasten them as required. A pole can always be got; it is needless to carry them.

I would advise a large party taking several of these tents instead of one large one. They are easier to carry about, and the party can separate, break itself into units, so to speak, for prospecting purposes. For a party of two a smaller tent will do. Tents should be provided before entry. Material for their construction is expensive, and the supply limited in that country. The cost of making them is also much more than here. If possible, have the door made mosquito-proof. This is easily done by attaching a piece of cotton gauze or very light cotton cloth to each side of the door, which can be folded together and tied up with tape fastened to the walls to support it. This will prove a great comfort. To exclude them effectually we must load down our sod cloth well, or they will make entry that way. They will get in in most surprising ways and places.

In conclusion, I would say, make your outfit as simple and serviceable as possible. Do not meddle with notions, designed to overcome this, that, or the other difficulty, as they very often create more trouble than that we take them to obviate. Metallic boats I would specially warn against. They may be light, capacious, and useful, but they are easily fractured and difficult to mend, while a wooden boat can be mended at almost any time and place, and breaks and fractures may be confidently looked forward to. If bass wood canoes are taken, some pieces of the planking should be taken along for mending with. Some rough lengths, which would not be of much service in the construction of a boat or canoe, can easily be carried in the bottom.

When a break is made in a canoe, if the parts are not too much fractured, they may be coated with white lead on the broken edges, pushed back to their original positions, a piece of the planking cut to overlap the fracture, coated with white lead, put over it on the inside and nailed and clinched tight to it. This makes it as strong as ever. Should the break be too bad to do this with, the fractured parts should be cut out neatly with a bevel on the cut edge; a piece of planking cut bevelled edge to fit this hole is put into it, after coating the edge with white lead, and another piece put over it on the inside, as before, so as to lap over the cut joint, and nailed and clinched, will make the boat as sound as new, and it is only the work of an hour or less.

MINING METHODS.

Bed-rock prospecting necessarily has to be reserved for the winter. First the moss has to be cleared away, and then the muck or decayed vegetable mould has to be picked away for a depth of two or three feet. After two or three feet in depth has been picked out, a fire is built in this 'hole,' as it is termed, in the evening. In the morning the ground which has been thawed by the fire is shovelled out, and in the afternoon wood for another fire procured; in the evening another fire is built, the ground thawed by this is the following morning shovelled out—and so on until bedrock is reached. Six, eight, ten, and twelve feet of the surface is decayed vegetable matter and alluvial deposit of sand in the clay, termed by the miners 'muck.' As soon as gravel is struck, prospecting is commenced—that is, a pan or two of the dirt is washed to determine whether it is worth keeping or not, as the refuse is thrown on one side of the hole, and the paying dirt on the other. Near to and on bed-rock the pay is found, which is generally not more than two or three feet deep. With reference to the so-called muck—all the way through it trees are found lying in every direction. These trees are of the same kinds of wood, and present the same appearances of growth as those to-day growing on the surface. The gold deposit, or pay dirt, was probably made thousands of years ago, yet in it we find the bones of animals which are still quite common in the district, and of others which are found farther to the south. Bedrock, and the gravel above it, show no evidence of glaciation; the gold itself bears no evidence of glaciation. Now, a few words on the manner of getting out the dirt in this region. As soon as the ground is sufficiently frozen to enable work to be started without interference from water, a hole is sunk to bedrock. The time this takes is measured by the depth of the hole, one foot per day being counted fair work. Should bed-rock be reached without finding prospects, another hole has to be sunk in the same way, and this process continued until pay is struck. One claim-holder may locate pay at the first hole; the man adjoining may have to sink many. The pay streak is seldom more than three feet in depth. On the side of the hole which shows the best indications a fire is placed, which thaws out a few inches on that wall to a height of forty-five feet. The pay dirt is placed in a 'dump,' and soon freezes solid. In this way the pay streak is taken from underneath.

A TABLE OF DISTANCES

FROM VARIOUS STARTING-POINTS TO THE KLONDYKE.

The following table of distances from Canadian points to Dawson City by the various routes will be of interest to intending gold-seekers:—

STRICKEEN ROUTE.

	Miles
Vancouver to Fort Wrangel (ocean)	700
Fort Wrangel to Glenora (river)	125
Glenora to Lake Teslin (trail or waggon)	145
Teslin to Fort Selkirk (lake and river)	400
Fort Selkirk to Stewart River (river)	105
Stewart River to Dawson City (river)	67
Total distance	1,542

DYEA AND CHILCOOT PASS.

	Miles
Vancouver to Dyea	995
Mouth of Canyon	8
Sheep Camp	3

A TABLE OF DISTANCES

Summit of Chilcoot Pass	4
Crater Lake	1
Lake Lindermann Landing	9.25
Foot of Lake Lindermann	4.45
Head of Lake Bennett	0.60
Boundary line between B. C. and N. W. T.	10
Foot of Lake Bennett	15.76
Caribou Crossing (Lake Nares)	2.59
Foot of Tagish Lake	16.81
Head of Marsh Lake	4.90
Foot of Marsh Lake	19.06
Head of Canyon	25.73
Foot of Canyon	0.62
Head of White Horse Rapids	0.39
Foot of White Horse Rapids	0.38
Head of Lake Lebarge	13.15
Foot of Lake Lebarge	31.16
Hootalinqua (Teslin) River	31.66
Big Salmon River	33.45
Little Salmon River	36.21
Five Fingers Rapids	59.29
Pelly River	58.46
White River	95.80
Sixty-Mile Creek	21.50
Dawson City	45.29
Total distance	1,372.89

APPENDIX

DALTON TRAIL.

	Miles
Vancouver to Chilcat Inlet	1,000
Chilcat Inlet to Fort Selkirk	300
Fort Selkirk to Dawson City	172
Total distance	1,472

SKAGUAY ROUTE.

	Miles
Vancouver to Skaguay (water)	995
Skaguay to Tagish Lake (pack trail)	66
Tagish Lake to Dawson City, same as Dyea route	520
Total distance	1,581

ST. MICHAEL'S ROUTE.

	Miles
Vancouver to St. Michael's (ocean)	2,800
St. Michael's to Dawson City (river)	1,650
Total distance	4,450

EDMONTON ROUTE.

	Miles
Edmonton to Athabasca Landing (waggon)	90
Athabasca Landing to Grand Rapids (river)	167
Grand Rapids to Fort McMurray (river)	87
Fort McMurray to Smith's Landing (river)	287
Smith's Landing to Fort Smith (river)	16

A TABLE OF DISTANCES

	Miles
Fort Smith to Fort Resolution (river)	194
Fort Resolution to Fort Providence (river)	168
Fort Providence to Fort Simpson (river)	161
Fort Simpson to Fort Wrigley (river)	136
Fort Wrigley to Fort Norman (river)	184
Fort Norman to Fort Good Hope (river)	174
Fort Good Hope to Fort Macpherson (river)	60
Fort Macpherson to Lapierre House (river)	250
Lapierre House to the Porcupine (trail)	20
Porcupine to Fort Yukon (river)	400
Fort Yukon to Dawson City (river)	303
Total distance	2,697

PRINCE ALBERT ROUTE.

	Miles
Prince Albert to Green Lake (waggon)	140
Green Lake to Portage la Roche (river)	220
Portage la Roche to Clearwater River (road)	12
Clearwater River to Fort McMurray (river)	80
Fort McMurray to Dawson City (river and trail) (Via Fort Macpherson and Porcupine river, same as Edmonton route)	2,
Total distance	2,805

EDMONTON-PEACE RIVER ROUTE.

	Miles
Edmonton to Peace River Crossing (trail)	260
Crossing to Forks at Nelson (trail)	240

APPENDIX

	Miles
Down Nelson to Liard (river)	120
Up Liard to Dease (river and trail)	160
Dease River to Pelly River (river and trail)	170
Pelly River to Fort Selkirk	220
Fort Selkirk to Dawson City	172
Total distance	1,342

ASHCROFT.

	Miles
Ashcroft to Quesnelle (stage)	220
Quesnelle to Hazleton, on the Skeona River (trail)	300
Hazleton to Telegraph Creek (trail)	240
Telegraph Creek to Teslin Lake (trail)	145
Teslin Lake to Dawson City (lake and river)	572
Total distance	1,477

REGULATIONS

GOVERNING PLACER MINING IN THE PROVISIONAL DISTRICT OF YUKON, NORTH-WEST TERRITORIES

(Approved by Order in Council of January 18th, 1898.)

INTERPRETATION.

'Free Miner' shall mean a male or female over the age of eighteen, but not under that age; or joint stock company, named in, and lawfully possessed of, a valid existing free miner's certificate, and no other.

'Legal post' shall mean a stake standing not less than four feet above the ground, and flatted on two sides for at least one foot from the top. Both sides so flatted shall measure at least four inches across the face. It shall also mean any stump or tree cut off and flatted or faced to the above height and size.

'Close season' shall mean the period of the year during which placer mining is generally suspended. The period to be fixed by the Mining Recorder in whose district the claim is situated.

'Mineral' shall include all minerals whatsoever other than coal.

'Joint Stock Company' shall mean any company incorporated for mining purposes under a Canadian charter, or licensed by the Government of Canada.

'Mining Recorder' shall mean the official appointed by the Gold Commissioner to record applications and grant entries for claims in the Mining Divisions into which the Commissioner may divide the Yukon District.

FREE MINERS AND THEIR PRIVILEGES.

1. Every person over, but not under eighteen years of age, and every joint stock company, shall be entitled to all the rights and privileges of a free miner, under these regulations and under the regulations governing

quartz mining, and shall be considered a free miner upon taking out a free miner's certificate. A free miner's certificate issued to a joint stock company shall be issued in its corporate name. A free miner's certificate shall not be transferable.

2. A free miner's certificate may be granted for one year to run from the date thereof or from the expiration of the applicant's then existing certificate, upon the payment therefor of the sum of ten dollars, unless the certificate is to be issued in favour of a joint stock company, in which case the fee shall be fifty dollars for a company having a nominal capital of one hundred thousand dollars or less, and for a company having a nominal capital exceeding one hundred thousand dollars, the fee shall be one hundred dollars. Only one person or joint stock company shall be named in the certificate.

3. A free miner's certificate shall be on the following form:

DOMINION OF CANADA.

FREE MINER'S CERTIFICATE.

(Non-transferable.)

Date................   No......

Valid for one year only.

This is to certify that.............. of .... has paid me this day the sum of........... and is entitled to all the rights and privileges of a free miner, under any mining regulations of the Government of Canada, for one year from the....... day of .... 18 ...

This certificate shall also grant to the holder thereof the privilege of fishing and shooting, subject to the provisions of any Act which has been passed, or which may hereafter be passed for the protection of game and fish; also the privilege of cutting timber for actual necessities, for building houses, boats, and for general mining operations; such timber, however, to be for the exclusive use of the miner himself, but such permission shall not extend to timber which may have been heretofore or which may hereafter be granted to other persons or corporations.

4. Free miner's certificates may be obtained by applicants in person at the Department of the Interior, Ottawa, or from the agents of Dominion Lands at Winnipeg, Manitoba; Calgary, Edmonton, Prince Albert, in the Northwest Territories; Kamloops and New Westminster, in the Province of British Columbia; at Dawson City, in the Yukon District; also from agents of the Government at Vancouver and Victoria, British Columbia, and at other places which may from time to time be named by the Minister of the Interior.

5. If any person or joint stock company shall apply for a free miner's certificate at the agent's office during his absence, and shall leave the fee required by these regulations with the officer or other person in charge of said office, he or it shall be entitled to have such certificate from the date of such applica-

tion; and any free miner shall at any time be entitled to obtain a free miner's certificate commencing to run from the expiration of his then existing free miner's certificate, provided that when he applies for such certificate he shall produce to the agent, or in case of his absence shall leave with the officer or other person in charge of the agent's office, such existing certificate.

6. If any free miner's certificate be accidentally destroyed or lost, the owner thereof may, on payment of a fee of two dollars, have a true copy of it, signed by the agent, or other person by whom or out of whose office the original was issued. Every such copy shall be marked 'Substituted Certificate'; and unless some material irregularity be shown in respect thereof, every original or substituted free miner's certificate shall be evidence of all matters therein contained.

7. No person or joint stock company will be recognized as having any right or interest in or to any placer claim, quartz claim, min-

ing lease, bed-rock flume grand, or any minerals in any ground comprised therein, or in or to any water right, mining ditch, drain, tunnel, or flume, unless he or it and every person in his or its employment shall have a free miner's certificate unexpired. And on the expiration of a free miner's certificate the owner thereof shall absolutely forfeit all his rights and interest in or to any placer claim, mining lease, bed-rock flume grant, and any minerals in any ground comprised therein, and in or to any and every water right, mining ditch, drain, tunnel, or flume, which may be held or claimed by such owner of such expired free miner's certificate, unless such owner shall, on or before the day following the expiration of such certificate, obtain a new free miner's certificate. Provided, nevertheless, that should any co-owner fail to keep up his free miner's certificate, such failure shall not cause a forfeiture or act as an abandonment of the claim, but the interest of the co-owner who shall fail to keep up his free miner's certificate, shall, *ipso facto*, be and become vested in his co-owners, *pro rata*, according to their former interests; provided, nevertheless, that a shareholder in a joint stock company need not be a free miner, and, though not a free miner, shall be entitled to buy, sell, hold, or dispose of any shares therein.

8. Every free miner shall, during the continuance of his certificate, but not longer, have the right to enter, locate, prospect, and mine for gold and other minerals upon any lands in the Yukon District, whether vested in the Crown or otherwise, except upon Government reservations for town sites, land which is occupied by any building, and any land falling within the curtilage of any dwelling house, and any land lawfully occupied for placer mining purposes, and also Indian reservations.

9. Previous to any entry being made upon lands lawfully occupied, such free miner shall give adequate security to the satisfaction of the Mining Recorder, for any loss or damage which may be caused by such entry; and after such entry he shall make full com-

pensation to the occupant or owner of such lands for any loss or damage which may be caused by reason of such entry; such compensation, in case of dispute, to be determined by a court having jurisdiction in mining disputes with or without a jury.

NATURE AND SIZE OF CLAIMS

10. A creek or gulch claim shall be two hundred and fifty feet long measured in the general direction of the creek or gulch. The boundaries of the claim which run in the general direction of the creek or gulch shall be lines along bed or rim rock three feet higher than the rim or edge of the creek, or the lowest general level of the gulch within the claim, so drawn or marked as to be at every point three feet above the rim or edge of the creek or the lowest general level of the gulch, opposite to it at right angles to the general direction of the claim for its length, but such boundaries shall not in any case exceed one thousand feet on each side of the centre

of the stream or gulch. (See Diagram No. 1.)

11. If the boundaries be less than one hundred feet apart horizontally, they shall be lines traced along bed or rim rock one hundred feet apart horizontally, following as nearly as practicable the direction of the valley for the length of the claim. (See Diagram No. 2.)

12. A river claim shall be situated only on one side of the river, and shall not exceed two hundred and fifty feet in length, measured in the general direction of the river. The other boundary of the claim which runs in the general direction of the river shall be lines along bed or rim rock three feet higher than the rim or edge of the river within the claim, so drawn or marked as to be at every point three feet above the rim or edge of the river opposite to it at right angles to the general direction of the claim for its length; but such boundaries shall not in any case be less than two hundred and fifty feet, or exceed a distance of one thousand feet from low water mark of the river. (See Diagram No. 3.)

DIAGRAM No. 1

PLAN OF CREEK OR GULCH CLAIM

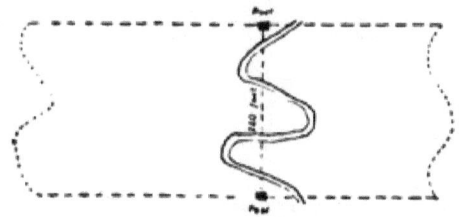

SECTIONAL PLAN OF A CREEK CLAIM.

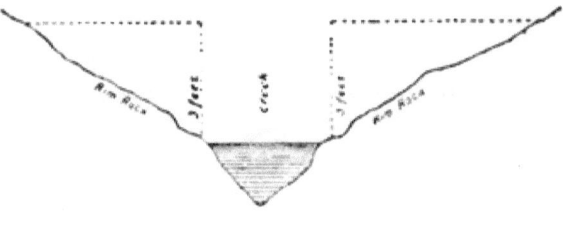

SECTIONAL PLAN OF A GULCH CLAIM

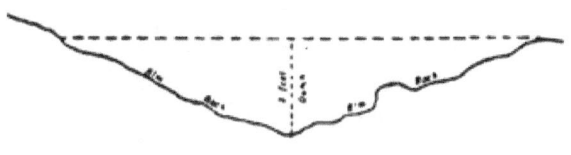

DIAGRAM No. 2.
PLAN SHEWING SIDE BOUNDARIES LESS THAN 100 FEET APART

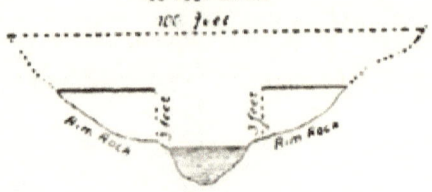

DIAGRAM No. 3.
SECTIONAL PLAN OF A RIVER CLAIM.

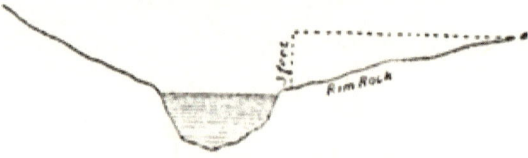

DIAGRAM No. 4.
SHOWING HOW CLAIMS ARE TO BE STAKED.
PLAN OF A CREEK OR GULCH CLAIM

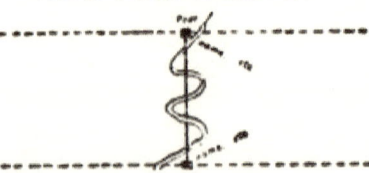

PLAN OF A RIVER CLAIM.

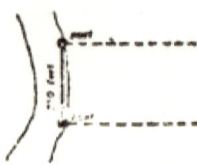

13. A 'hill claim' shall not exceed two hundred and fifty feet in length, drawn parallel to the main direction of the stream or ravine on which it fronts. Parallel lines drawn from each end of the base line at right angles thereto, and running to the summit of the hill (provided the distance does not exceed one thousand feet), shall constitute the end boundaries of the claim.

14. All other placer claims shall be two hundred and fifty feet square.

15. Every placer claim shall be as nearly as possible rectangular in form, and marked by two legal posts firmly fixed in the ground in the manner shown in diagram No. 4. The line between the two posts shall be well cut out so that one post may, if the nature of the surface will permit, be seen from the other. The flatted side of each post shall face the claim, and on each post shall be written, on the side facing the claim, a legible notice stating the name or number of the claim, or both if possible, its length in feet, the date when staked, and the full Christian and surname of the locator.

16. Every alternate ten claims shall be reserved for the Government of Canada. That is to say, when a claim is located, the discoverer's claim and nine additional claims adjoining each other, and numbered consecutively, will be open for registration. Then the next ten claims of two hundred and fifty feet each will be reserved for the Government, and so on. The alternate group of claims reserved for the Crown shall be disposed of in such manner as may be decided by the Minister of the Interior.

17. The penalty for trespassing upon a claim reserved for the Crown shall be immediate cancellation by the Mining Recorder of any entry or entries which the person trespassing may have obtained, whether by original entry or purchase, for a mining claim, and the refusal by the Mining Recorder of the acceptance of any application which the person trespassing may at any time make for a claim. In addition to such penalty, the Mounted Police, upon a requisition from the Mining Recorder to that

effect, shall take the necessary steps to eject the trespasser.

18. In defining the size of claims, they shall be measured horizontally, irrespective of inequalities on the surface of the ground.

19. If any free miner or party of free miners discover a new mine, and such discovery shall be established to the satisfaction of the Mining Recorder, creek, river or hill, claims of the following size shall be allowed, namely :—

To one discoverer, one claim, five hundred feet in length.

To a party of two discoverers, two claims, amounting together to one thousand feet in length.

To each member of a party beyond two in number, a claim of the ordinary size only.

20. A new stratum of auriferous earth or gravel situated in a locality where the claims have been abandoned shall for this purpose be deemed a new mine, although the same locality shall have been previously worked at a different level.

21. The forms of application for a grant for placer mining, and the grant of the same, shall be those contained in Forms 'H' and 'I' in the schedule hereto.

22. A claim shall be recorded with the Mining Recorder in whose district it is situated within ten days after the location thereof, if it is located within ten miles of the Mining Recorder's office. One extra day shall be allowed for every additional ten miles or fraction thereof.

23. In the event of the claim being more than one hundred miles from a Recorder's office, and situated where other claims are being located, the free miners, not less than five in number, are authorized to meet and appoint one of their number a 'Free Miners' Recorder,' who shall act in that capacity until a Mining Recorder is appointed by the Gold Commissioner.

24. The 'Free Miners' Recorder' shall, at the earliest possible date after his appointment, notify the nearest Government Mining Recorder thereof, and upon the arrival of the

Government Mining Recorder he shall deliver to him his records and the fees received for recording the claims. The Government Mining Recorder shall then grant to each free miner whose name appears in the records, an entry for his claim on form 'I' of these regulations, provided an application has been made by him in accordance with form 'H' thereof. The entry to date from the time the 'Free Miners' Recorder' recorded the application.

25. If the 'Free Miners' Recorder' fails within three months to notify the nearest Government Mining Recorder of his appointment, the claims which he may have recorded will be cancelled.

26. During the absence of the Mining Recorder from his office, the entry for a claim may be granted by any person whom he may appoint to perform his duties in his absence.

27. Entry shall not be granted for a claim which has not been staked by the applicant in person in the manner specified in these regulations. An affidavit that the claim was staked

out by the applicant shall be embodied in form 'H' in the schedule hereto.

28. An entry fee of fifteen dollars shall be charged the first year, and an annual fee of fifteen dollars for each of the following years. This provision shall apply to claims for which entries have already been granted.

29. A statement of the entries granted and fees collected shall be rendered by the Mining Recorder to the Gold Commissioner at least every three months, which shall be accompanied by the amount collected.

30. A royalty of ten per cent. on the gold mined shall be levied and collected on the gross output of each claim. The royalty may be paid at banking offices to be established under the auspices of the Government of Canada, or to the Gold Commissioner, or to any Mining Recorder authorized by him. The sum of two thousand five hundred dollars shall be deducted from the gross annual output of a claim when estimating the amount upon which royalty is to be calculated, but this exemption

shall not be allowed unless the royalty is paid at a banking office or to the Gold Commissioner or Mining Recorder. When the royalty is paid monthly or at longer periods, the deduction shall be made ratable on the basis of two thousand five hundred dollars per annum for the claim. If not paid to the bank, Gold Commissioner, or Mining Recorder, it shall be collected by the customs officials or police officers when the miner passes the posts established at the boundary of a district. Such royalty to form part of the consolidated revenue, and to be accounted for by the officers who collect the same in due course. The time and manner in which such royalty shall be collected shall be provided for by regulations to be made by the Gold Commissioner.

31. Default in payment of such royalty, if continued for ten days after notice has been posted on the claim in respect of which it is demanded, or in the vicinity of such claim, by the Gold Commissioner or his agent, shall be followed by cancellation of the claim. Any

attempt to defraud the Crown by withholding any part of the revenue thus provided for, by making false statements of the amount taken out, shall be punished by cancellation of the claim in respect of which fraud or false statements have been committed or made. In respect to the facts as to such fraud or false statements or non-payment of royalty, the decision of the Gold Commissioner shall be final.

32. After the recording of a claim the removal of any post by the holder thereof, or by any person acting in his behalf for the purpose of changing the boundaries of his claim, shall act as a forfeiture of the claim.

33. The entry of every holder of a grant for placer mining must be renewed and his receipt relinquished and replaced every year, the entry fee being paid each time.

34. The holder of a creek, gulch, or river claim may, within sixty days after staking out the claim, obtain an entry for a hill claim adjoining it, by paying to the Mining Recorder the sum of one hundred dollars. This per-

mission shall also be given to the holder of a creek, gulch, or river claim obtained under former regulations, provided that the hill claim is available at the time an application is made therefor.

35. No miner shall receive a grant of more than one mining claim in a mining district, the boundaries of which shall be defined by the Mining Recorder, but the same miner may also hold a hill claim, acquired by him under these regulations in connection with a creek, gulch, or river claim, and any number of claims by purchase ; and any number of miners may unite to work their claims in common, upon such terms as they may arrange, provided such agreement is registered with the Mining Recorder and a fee of five dollars paid for each registration.

36. Any free miner or miners may sell, mortgage, or dispose of his or their claims, provided such disposal be registered with, and a fee of two dollars paid to the Mining Recorder, who shall thereupon give the

assignee a certificate in the form 'J' in the schedule hereto.

37. Every free miner shall, during the continuance of his grant, have the exclusive right of entry upon his own claim for the miner-like working thereof, and the construction of a residence thereon, and shall be entitled exclusively to all the proceeds realized therefrom, upon which, however, the royalty prescribed by these regulations shall be payable; provided that the Mining Recorder may grant to the holders of other claims such right of entry thereon as may be absolutely necessary for the working of their claims, upon such terms as may to him seem reasonable. He may also grant permits to miners to cut timber thereon for their own use.

39. Every free miner shall be entitled to the use of so much of the water naturally flowing through or past his claim, and not already lawfully appropriated, as shall, in the opinion of the Mining Recorder, be necessary for the due working thereof, and shall be

entitled to drain his own claim free of charge.

39. A claim shall be deemed to be abandoned and open to occupation and entry by any person when the same shall have remained unworked on working days, excepting during the close season, by the grantee thereof, or by some person on his behalf, for the space of seventy-two * hours, unless sickness or other reasonable cause be shown to the satisfaction of the Mining Recorder, or unless the grantee is absent on leave given by the Mining Recorder; and the Mining Recorder, upon obtaining evidence satisfactory to himself, that this provision is not being complied with, may cancel the entry given for a claim.

40. If any cases arise for which no provision is made in these regulations, the provisions of the regulations governing the disposal of mineral lands other than coal

---

* Seventy-two hours means three consecutive days of twenty-four hours each.

lands, approved by His Excellency the Governor in Council on the 9th of November, 1889, or such other regulations as may be substituted therefor, shall apply.

FORM H.—APPLICATION FOR GRANT FOR PLACER MINING, AND AFFIDAVIT OF APPLICANT.

I (or we) .... of .... hereby apply, under the Yukon Placer Mining Regulations, for a grant of a claim for placer mining as defined in the said regulations, in (here describe locality) and I (or we) solemnly swear :—

1. That from indications I (or we) have observed on the claim applied for, I (or we) have reason to believe that there is therein a deposit of gold.

2. That I (or we) am (or are) to the best of my (or our) knowledge and belief the first to observe such indications, or :—

3. That the said claim was previously granted to (here name the last grantee), but has remained unworked by the said grantee for not less than . . . .

4. That I (or we) am (or are) unaware that the land is other than vacant Dominion Lands.

5. That I (or we) did on the . . . . day of . . . . mark out on the ground, in accordance in every particular with the provisions of the mining regulations for the Yukon District, the claim for which I (or we) make this application, and in so doing I (or we) did not encroach on any other claim or mining location previously laid out by any other person.

6. That the length of the said claim, as nearly as I (or we) could measure, is . . . . feet, and that the description of this date hereto attached, signed by me (or us) sets (or set) forth in detail, to the best of my (or our) knowledge and ability, its position.

7. That I (or we) make this application in

good faith, to acquire the claim for the sole purpose of mining to be prosecuted by myself (or us) or by myself and associates, or by my (or our) assigns.

Sworn before me
at ....
this .... day   (Signature)
of .... 18 ...

FORM I.—GRANT FOR PLACER MINING.

No. ......

    Department of the Interior,

        Agency .... 18 ......

In consideration of the payment of the fee of fifteen dollars prescribed by clause 28 of the mining regulations for the Yukon District, by .... (A. B.) .... of .... accompanying his (or their) application No. .... dated .... 18 ..., for a mining claim in .... (here insert description of locality).

The Minister of Interior hereby grants to

the said .... (A. B.) ...... for the term of one year from the date hereof, the exclusive right of entry upon the claim .... (here describe in detail the claim granted) for the miner-like working thereof, and the construction of a residence thereon, and the exclusive right to all the proceeds realized therefrom, upon which, however, the royalty prescribed by the regulations shall be paid.

The said .... (A. B.) .... shall be entitled to the use of so much of the water naturally flowing through or past his (or their) claim, and not already lawfully appropriated, as shall be necessary for the due working thereof, and to drain his (or their) claim, free of charge.

This grant does not convey to the said .... (A. B.) ...... any right of ownership in the soil covered by the said claim, and the said grant shall lapse and be forfeited unless the claim is continuously and in good faith worked by the said ...... (A. B.) ...... or his (or their) associates.

The rights hereby granted are those laid down in the aforesaid mining regulations, and no more, and are subject to all the provisions of the said regulations, whether the same are expressed herein or not.

....
Mining Recorder.

FORM J.—CERTIFICATE OF THE ASSIGNMENT OF A PLACER MINING CLAIM.

No.......

Department of the Interior,

Agency............18......

This is to certify that...... (B. C.)...... of...... has (or have) filed an assignment in due form dated...... 18..., and accompanied by a registration fee of two dollars, of the grant to...... (A. B.)...... of....... of the right to mine in...... (here insert description of claim)..... for one year from the ...... 18....

This certificate entitles the said .... (B. C.) ..... to all the rights and privileges of the said ...... (A. B.) ...... in respect to the claim assigned, that is to say, to the exclusive right of entry upon the said claim for the miner-like working thereof, and the construction of a residence thereon, and the exclusive right to all the proceeds realized therefrom (upon which, however, the royalty prescribed by the regulations shall be paid) for the remaining portion of the year for which the said claim was granted to the said ...... (A. B.) ...... that is to say, until the ...... day of ...... 18 ....

The said ...... (B. C.) ...... shall be entitled to the use of so much of the water naturally flowing through or past his (or their) claim, and not already lawfully appropriated, as shall be necessary for the due working thereof, and to drain his claim, free of charge.

This grant does not convey to the said .... (B. C.) ...... any right of ownership in the soil covered by the said claim, and the said grant shall lapse and be forfeited unless the claim is continuously and in good faith worked by the said ......(B. C.)...... or his (or their) associates.

The rights hereby granted are those laid down in the Yukon Placer Mining Regulations, and no more, and are subject to all the provisions of the said regulations, whether the same are expressed herein or not.

....
Mining Recorder.

REGULATIONS

GOVERNING THE ISSUE OF LEASES TO DREDGE FOR MINERALS IN THE BEDS OF RIVERS IN THE PROVISIONAL DISTRICT OF YUKON, NORTH-WEST TERRITORIES.

(Approved of by Order in Council No. 125, of the 18th Jan., 1898.)

THE following regulations are adopted for the issue of leases to persons or companies who have obtained a free miner's certificate in accordance with the provisions of the regulations governing placer mining in the Provisional District of Yukon, to dredge for minerals other than coal in the submerged beds or bars of rivers in the Provisional District of Yukon, in the North-west Territories:

1. The lessee shall be given the exclusive

right to subaqueous mining and dredging for all minerals with the exception of coal in and along an unbroken extent of five miles of a river following its sinuosities, to be measured down the middle thereof, and to be described by the lessee in such manner as to be easily traced on the ground; and although the lessee may also obtain as many as five other leases, each for an unbroken extent of five miles of a river, so measured and described, no more than six such leases will be issued in favour of an individual or company, so that the maximum extent of river in and along which any individual or company shall be given the exclusive right above mentioned, shall under no circumstances exceed thirty miles. The lease shall provide for the survey of the leasehold under instructions from the Surveyor General, and for the filing of the returns of survey in the Department of the Interior within one year from the date of the lease.

2. The lease shall be for a term of twenty

years, at the end of which time all rights vested in, or which may be claimed by the lessee under his lease, are to cease and determine. The lease may be renewable, however, from time to time thereafter in the discretion of the Minister of the Interior.

3. The lessee's right of mining and dredging shall be confined to the submerged beds or bars in the river below water-mark, that boundary to be fixed by its position on the first day of August in the year of the date of the lease.

4. The lease shall be subject to the rights of all persons who have received or who may receive entries for claims under the Placer Mining Regulations.

5. The lessee shall have at least one dredge in operation upon the five miles of river leased to him, within two seasons from the date of his lease, and if, during one season when operations can be carried on, he fails to efficiently work the same to the satisfaction of the Minister of the Interior, the lease shall become null and

void unless the Minister of the Interior shall otherwise decide. Provided that when any company or individual has obtained more than one lease, one dredge for each fifteen miles or portion thereof shall be held to be compliance with this regulation.

6. The lessee shall pay a rental of one hundred dollars per annum for each mile of river so leased to him. The lessee shall also pay to the Crown a royalty of ten per centum on the output in excess of fifteen thousand dollars, as shown by sworn returns to be furnished monthly by the lessee to the Gold Commissioner, during the period that dredging operations are being carried on; such royalty, if any, to be paid with each return.

7. The lessee who is the holder of more than one lease shall be entitled to the exemption as to royalty provided for by the next preceding regulation to the extent of fifteen thousand dollars for each five miles of river for which he is the holder of a lease; but the lessee under one lease shall not be entitled to

the exemption as to the royalty provided by the next two preceding regulations, where the dredge or dredges used by him have been used in dredging by another lessee, or in any case in respect of more than thirty miles.

8. The lessee shall be permitted to cut free of all dues, on any land belonging to the Crown, such timber as may be necessary for the purposes of his lease, but such permission shall not extend to timber which may have been heretofore or may hereafter be granted to other persons or corporations.

9. The lessee shall not interfere in any way with the general right of the public to use the river in which he may be permitted to dredge, for navigation or other purposes; the free navigation of the river shall not be impeded by the deposit of tailings in such manner as to form bars or banks in the channel thereof, and the current or stream shall not be obstructed in any material degree by the accumulation of such deposits.

10. The lease shall provide that any person

who has received or may receive entry under the Placer Mining Regulations shall be entitled to run tailings into the river at any point thereon, and to construct all works which may be necessary for properly operating and working his claim. Provided that it shall not be lawful for such person to construct a wing-dam within one thousand feet from the place where any dredge is being operated, nor to obstruct or interfere in any way with the operation of any dredge.

11. The lease shall reserve all roads, ways, bridges, drains, and other public works, and all improvements now existing, or which may hereafter be made, in, upon, or under any part of the river, and the power to enter and construct the same, and shall provide that the lessee shall not damage or obstruct any public ways, drains, bridges, works and improvements now or hereafter to be made upon, in, over, through, or under the river; and that he will substantially bridge or cover and protect all the cuts, flumes, ditches, and sluices, and all

pits and dangerous places at all points where they may be crossed by a public highway or frequented path or trail, to the satisfaction of the Minister of the Interior.

12. That the lessee, his executors, administrators, or assigns shall not nor will assign, transfer, or sublet the demised premises, or any part thereof, without the consent in writing of the Minister first had and obtained.

TIMBER REGULATIONS

For the benefit of those English Corporations who purpose operating in Timber, these are the latest Government regulations :

REGULATIONS UNDER WHICH LICENSES TO CUT TIMBER ON DOMINION LANDS IN THE PROVISIONAL DISTRICT OF YUKON, NORTH-WEST TERRITORIES, MAY BE GRANTED.

1. A license to cut timber may be issued to any person who is the first applicant therefor, or it may be acquired at competition, as the Minister of the Interior may direct.

2. A bonus of not less than two hundred and fifty dollars shall be paid for each square mile to be licensed.

3. The area of a berth shall not exceed five square miles, and a berth shall not be less than one mile in breadth.

4. Not more than five berths of five square miles in the Provisional District of Yukon shall be granted to any one person or company.

5. A license to cut timber on a berth shall be issued yearly.

6. The licensee shall erect a saw-mill within a certain period to be fixed by the Minister of the Interior.

7. The licensee shall pay a stumpage of two dollars per thousand feet B. M. for the timber cut.

8. The licensee shall file in the Department of the Interior the returns of the survey of his berth when called upon by the Minister of the Interior to do so.

THE END.

London: Printed by Duncan Macdonald, Blenheim House, W.

NEW WORK BY W. A. PICKERING, C.M.G.

In One Vol. Demy 8vo, with Twenty-five Illustrations, from Photographs and Sketches by the Author, price 16s.

PIONEERING IN FORMOSA

RECOLLECTIONS OF ADVENTURES

AMONG

MANDARINS, WRECKERS, & HEAD-HUNTING SAVAGES

BY

W. A. PICKERING, C.M.G.

LATE PROTECTOR OF CHINESE IN THE STRAITS SETTLEMENTS

WITH AN APPENDIX
ON BRITISH POLICY AND INTERESTS IN CHINA
AND THE FAR EAST

LONDON: HURST AND BLACKETT, LIMITED.

NEW WORK BY DR. PARKER

Now Ready, at all Booksellers' and Libraries, in One Volume Crown 8vo. Price 3s. 6d.

CHRISTIAN PROFILES
IN A PAGAN MIRROR

BY

JOSEPH PARKER, D.D.
Minister of the City Temple, London.

An enlightened pagan lady comes to England to acquaint herself with the beliefs, the habits, and the customs of Christians. She has long been asking herself such questions as, Who are the Christians? What do they believe? What life do they lead? How do they conduct themselves towards each other? Having made inquiry and received impressions, she reports to a friend in India.

'It is a long time since the basis and elements of Christianity have been expounded so simply and effectively as in this instance. These "Christian Profiles" might well be submitted to those young people—and some of their elders also—who have yet to obtain an intelligent conception of the Christian faith. The volume has no sectarian bias, it deals with the fundamentals of Christianity, and should be applauded, therefore, as readily and strongly by Churchmen as by Nonconformists. It is calculated to be of real service to religion.'—*Globe.*

'These letters of a pagan lady expound the central doctrines of Christianity with a freshness and simplicity in which they are allowed to lose nothing of their force or persuasiveness. The book is eminently readable.'—*Scotsman.*

LONDON : HURST AND BLACKETT, LIMITED.

NEW WORK BY MR. MACKENZIE BELL

THIRD EDITION now ready, at all Booksellers' and Libraries, in 1 vol. demy 8vo, with Portraits and Facsimiles, extra cloth. 12s.

CHRISTINA ROSSETTI
A Biographical and Critical Study

By MACKENZIE BELL

Author of 'Spring's Immortality, and other Poems,'
'Charles Whitehead: a Biographical and Critical Monograph,' &c.

This is, in effect, the Authorised Life of the Poetess, being based largely on information and letters supplied by her relatives and intimate friends.

Under the Especial Patronage of Her Majesty.

SIXTY-SEVENTH YEAR OF PUBLICATION

Now Ready. In 1 vol. royal 8vo, with the Arms beautifully engraved, extra cloth, gilt edges, price 31s. 6d.

LODGE'S
PEERAGE AND BARONETAGE
FOR 1898
CORRECTED BY THE NOBILITY.

LONDON: HURST AND BLACKETT, LIMITED

IN ONE VOLUME, DEMY 8VO.
WITH PORTRAIT OF AUTHOR. PRICE 12s.

An Old Soldier's Memories

By S. H. JONES-PARRY, J.P., D.L.
Late Captain Royal Dublin Fusiliers,
AUTHOR OF "MY JOURNEY ROUND THE WORLD."

CONTENTS.

Parentage and Education—India in 1849—Rangoon—Pegu—Second Defence of Pegu—March to Shoaygheen—Tonghoo—London 1854—The Crimea—Homeward Bound—Lucknow—Alumbagh—Home 1868.

IN ONE VOLUME, LARGE CROWN 8VO, GILT TOP.
WITH PORTRAIT OF LADY HAMILTON IN PHOTOGRAVURE. PRICE 6s.

Lady Hamilton and Lord Nelson

AN HISTORICAL BIOGRAPHY
Based on Letters and other Documents in the Morrison Collection.

BY JOHN CORDY JEAFFRESON,
AUTHOR OF "THE REAL LORD BYRON."

NEW EDITION, CONDENSED, REVISED, AND WITH MUCH NEW MATERIAL.

HURST AND BLACKETT, LIMITED,
13, GREAT MARLBOROUGH STREET, LONDON, W.

NEW AND POPULAR NOVELS

NEW AND ORIGINAL NOVEL BY ADELINE SERGEANT
Now first published in 1 vol. crown 8vo. 6s.
SECOND EDITION NOW READY

MISS BETTY'S MISTAKE. By ADELINE SERGEANT, Author of 'The Claim of Anthony Lockhart,' &c.

'"Miss Betty's Mistake" can unhesitatingly be entered upon that list which carries the names of Miss Sergeant's happiest efforts to amuse us by means of wholesome fiction. The story is cleverly arranged and capitally written.'—*Literary World.*

'The wholesome sweetness with which the tale is told, and the sensitiveness of touch displayed in the drawing of all the characters, make it pleasant to read.'—*Dundee Advertiser.*

MERESIA. By WINIFRED GRAHAM, Author of 'A Strange Solution,' &c. In 1 vol. crown 8vo. 6s.

'I will not divulge the plot, which is original and mystifies the reader. It is not an easy book to lay down when you have taken it up.'—*Queen.*

'There is much that is clever and original in Miss Winifred Graham's latest book. Meresia is an interesting and a lifelike character, and the two Spaniards, Aladros and Serano, are also well drawn. The book is well worth reading, if only for the picture it gives us of "the fascination of hate."'—*Daily Telegraph.*

THE CAPRICE OF JULIA. By LEWIS SERGEANT. Now ready, in 1 vol. crown 8vo. 6s.

'Its plot is good, the character of Julia herself is well realized and adequately portrayed, and many of the scenes interest and convince. Other characters besides Julia's are well imagined and carefully wrought, and the situations are well conceived and brought forth with no lack of strength in the creator or of success in the result. "The Caprice of Julia" is a book to be read.'—*Pall Mall Gazette.*

'There is plenty of imagination to be found in "The Caprice of Julia." Taking the book altogether, it is clever, well-written, and entertaining.—*Standard.*

A STORM-RENT SKY. Scenes of Love and Revolution. By M. BETHAM-EDWARDS, Author of 'Kitty,' 'Dr. Jacob,' 'Brother Gabriel,' &c. Second Edition now ready, in 1 vol. crown 8vo. 6s.

A great-nephew of Danton writes:—'Les mœurs de l'époque et du pays sont bien peintes. Le caractère et le patriotisme de mon illustre parent sont mis en relief et décrits d'une façon aussi remarquable que vraie.'
V. SARDIN, Arcis-sur-Aube, 13 March.

'A story of varied charm and more than usual interest.'—*Weekly Sun.*

'Prudent Parisse, the village schoolmaster, is an admirable creation.'—*Standard.*

LONDON : HURST AND BLACKETT, LIMITED

HURST AND BLACKETT'S
Half-a-Crown Series, in Red Cloth.

LIFE OF MARIE ANTOINETTE.
BY CHARLES DUKE YONGE.

| ADELE. | NATHALIE. |
| BY JULIA KAVANAGH. | BY JULIA KAVANAGH. |

THE CRESCENT AND THE CROSS.
BY ELIOT WARBURTON.

ST. OLAVE'S.
BY THE AUTHOR OF 'JANITA'S CROSS.'

| THE OLD COURT SUBURB. | ON THE SCENT. |
| BY LEIGH HUNT. | BY LADY M. MAJENDIE. |

GRANDMOTHER'S MONEY.
BY F. W. ROBINSON.

ADAM GRAEME OF MOSSGRAY.
BY MRS. OLIPHANT.

| BARBARA'S HISTORY. | THE LAIRD OF NORLAW. |
| BY AMELIA B. EDWARDS. | BY MRS. OLIPHANT. |

IT WAS A LOVER AND HIS LASS.
BY MRS. OLIPHANT.

| AGNES. | NO CHURCH. |
| BY MRS. OLIPHANT. | BY F. W. ROBINSON. |

LORD BRACKENBURY.
BY AMELIA B. EDWARDS, LL.D.

| A ROSE IN JUNE. | PHŒBE, JUNIOR. |
| BY MRS. OLIPHANT. | BY MRS. OLIPHANT. |

THROUGH THE LONG NIGHT.
BY MRS. E. LYNN LINTON.

LIFE OF THE REV. EDWARD IRVING.
BY MRS. OLIPHANT.

MARGARET AND HER BRIDESMAIDS.
BY THE AUTHOR OF 'THE VALLEY OF A HUNDRED FIRES.'

THE VALLEY OF A HUNDRED FIRES.
BY THE AUTHOR OF 'MARGARET AND HER BRIDESMAIDS.'

LONDON: HURST AND BLACKETT, LIMITED.

The only Authorized Editions

OF

'JOHN HALIFAX, GENTLEMAN'

ILLUSTRATED EDITION

    Illustrations by Hugh Riviere, large crown 8vo, extra cloth, gilt top, price 6s.

STANDARD EDITION

    Crown 8vo, cloth, with frontispiece by Sir John Millais, Bart., price 5s.

TEWKESBURY EDITION

    Crown 8vo, cloth, with portrait of Author by Professor Herkomer, cloth, price 3s. 6d.

POPULAR EDITION

    Crown 8vo, cloth, price 2s.

PEOPLE'S EDITION

    In medium 8vo, cloth, price 1s.

    In paper cover, price 6d.

LONDON: HURST AND BLACKETT, LIMITED.

BEATRICE WHITBY'S NOVELS.

EACH IN ONE VOLUME CROWN 8vo—3s. 6d.

THE AWAKENING OF MARY FENWICK.

"We have no hesitation in declaring that 'The Awakening of Mary Fenwick' is the best novel of its kind that we have seen for some years. It is apparently a first effort, and, as such, is really remarkable. The story is extremely simple. Mary Mauser marries her husband for external, and perhaps rather inadequate, reasons, and then discovers that he married her because she was an heiress. She feels the indignity acutely, and does not scruple to tell him her opinion—her very candid opinion—of his behaviour. That is the effect of the first few chapters, and the rest of Miss Whitby's book is devoted to relating how this divided couple hated, quarrelled, and finally fell in love with one another. Mary Fenwick and her husband live and move and make us believe in them in a way which few but the great masters of fiction have been able to compass."—*Athenæum.*

ONE REASON WHY.

"The governess makes a re-entry into fiction under the auspices of Beatrice Whitby in 'One Reason Why.' Readers generally, however, will take a great deal more interest, for once, in the children than in their instructress. 'Pay' and 'Ellie' are charmingly natural additions to the children of novel-land; so much so, that there is a period when one dreads a death-bed scene for one of them—a fear which is happily unfulfilled.—*Graphic.*

PART OF THE PROPERTY.

'The book is a thoroughly good one. The theme is fairly familiar—the rebellion of a spirited girl against a match which has been arranged for her without her knowledge or consent; her resentment at being treated, not as a woman with a heart and will, but as 'part of the property;' and her final discovery, which is led up to with real dramatic skill, that the thing against which her whole nature had risen in revolt has become the one desire of her heart. The author's greatest triumph is the portrait of Mrs Lindsay, who, with the knowledge of the terrible skeleton in the cupboard of her apparently happy home, wears so bravely the mask of light gaiety as to deceive everybody but the one man who knows her secret."—*Spectator.*

IN THE SUNTIME OF HER YOUTH.

'A description of a home stripped by the cold wind of poverty of all its comforts, but which remains home still. The careless optimism of the head of the family would be incredible, if we did not know how men exist full of responsibilities yet free from solicitudes, and who tread with a jaunty step the very verge of ruin; his inconsolable widow would be equally improbable, if we did not meet every day with women who devote themselves to such idols of clay. There is interest in it from first to last, and its pathos is relieved by touches of true humour."—*Illustrated London News*

MARY FENWICK'S DAUGHTER.

"This is one of the most delightful novels we have read for a long time. 'Bab' Fenwick is an 'out of doors' kind of girl, full of spirit, wit, go, and sin, both original and acquired. Her lover, Jack, is all that a hero should be, and great and magnanimous as he is, finds some difficulty in forgiving the *insouciante* mistress all her little sins of omission and commission. When she finally shoots him in the leg—by accident—the real tragedy of the story begins. The whole is admirable."—*Black and White.*

A MATTER OF SKILL.

"Lovely woman appears in these pages in a variety of moods, humorous and pathetic, and occasionally she seems not a little 'uncertain, coy, and hard to please.' The title story, showing how a stately girl is captured, after a good deal of trouble, by a short and commonplace young man, is very amusing; and there are other sketches in which it is interesting to follow the wiles of Mother Eve ere she has come to years of discretion."—*Academy.*

LONDON : HURST AND BLACKETT, LIMITED.

www.ingramcontent.com/pod-product-compliance
Lightning Source LLC
Chambersburg PA
CBHW030751230426
43667CB00007B/923